BUILDING BLACK BUSINESS

An Analysis and a Plan

BUILDING BLACK BUSINESS
An Analysis and a Plan

ABRAHAM S. VENABLE

Earl G. Graves Publishing Co., Inc.
Distributed by Thomas Y. Crowell Company • New York

Designed by Virginia Smith

Manufactured in the United States of America

L.C. Card 72–78276
ISBN 0–690–16100–X

1 2 3 4 5 6 7 8 9 10

FOREWORD

Creating a successful business is one of the most difficult things that anyone ever sets out to do. But, like Abe Venable, I believe that the growth of a successful business community is an essential part of the development of the entire black community. Minorities must become more involved in business, for until we have the full participation of all minorities—and I'm thinking about Chicanos and Puerto Ricans and Indians and Orientals and others as well as black people—this will never be a truly strong nation. As long as there are people trapped in the cellar, America will not be a happy house. I hope that "Building Black Business" will help us reach that goal of full involvement for all of America's people.

What does it take to build a successful business community? It requires competence, of course. You simply can't run successful businesses without able and experienced people. But to me two of the most important components of a successful business community are trust and confidence. We must have trust and confidence in ourselves, trust and confidence in our fellow black people, and trust and confidence in the sincere goodwill of many white Americans. I'm not talking about blind faith, the kind of faith that we sometimes rely upon when we should be relying upon the advice of a good attorney. Too often we become involved in an enterprise simply because someone says, "You can trust me." That is the sort of assurance that has led many businessmen to financial ruin. I recall receiving a phone call several years ago from a New York district attorney. It seems that a doctor had invested $30,000 in a business because he was allegedly told that I had expressed my approval of the business. Without calling me or consulting a lawyer, the doctor went ahead and invested his money, and, in the end, he lost that investment. You can't assume that because you are honest, everybody else is going to be honest too.

The kind of trust that I am talking about is a much broader form of trust. It's a form of trust that is, at its foundation, not only sensible but also shrewd. It means that you don't reject a business opportunity simply because white people are involved in it. There are many white people who sincerely want to help. We have to use the expertise of white America, and we should use it without shame. For so many years white America used the labor of black America. Now it's time for black America to use the expertise of white America. We have the enthusiasm and many of the other essential ingredients for going into business, but we have to learn the necessary techniques and procedures of business that come from experience. And, by and large, the people who have that experience, who have developed and mastered those techniques and procedures, are white people. There is no disgrace in using white labor, and the success of a business is not diminished because that business is interracial.

While we must have faith in the goodwill and expertise of many white people, we will make little progress until we learn to have confidence in one another, to trust in one another, to believe in one another's abilities. We must recognize that black businessmen can and will come to grips with and solve the problems at hand, if given the chance. We must be more open with one another and one very tangible way that black businessmen can show confidence in one another is by doing business with one another.

Most important perhaps, we have to have confidence in ourselves as individuals. Frankly, when I first began in business I didn't have confidence in my own abilities. I didn't know whether I had the qualifications to succeed in business. And because I lacked that basic self-confidence I was often embarrassed to admit that I didn't understand the technical aspects of a discussion.

But I have discovered that people generally have more respect for you and are less likely to exploit you if you admit that you don't understand something. They are impressed that you have enough self-assurance to admit that you lack experience. And then, probably because there is some schoolteacher in all of us, the technician is usually proud to explain everything in useful detail.

Finally, we have to trust in the loyalty of the people who work for us, and I think that it makes good sense to encourage that loyalty by making it clear to employees that as the business grows their remuneration will grow with it.

The success of the black business community will depend, to a large degree, on the proper use of trust and cooperation. We succeeded in baseball because we had a lot of people working together. And we are going to succeed in business in the same way—through the efforts of a lot of people working together.

Jackie Robinson
New York, 1972

ACKNOWLEDGMENTS

I owe a great deal of thanks to the many people who assisted me in developing this book. First, I must offer special thanks to five of my former staff assistants at the Office of Minority Business Enterprise, U.S. Department of Commerce.

James Sexton, a treasured friend, had to listen to my many concerns about the book. He spent many hours from our college days at Howard University discussing my thoughts about black business. Al Horton, my former Special Assistant, is one of the best writers with whom I have had the pleasure of working. His assistance in smoothing out many rough segments of the book proved invaluable. Tim Ebenreiter, whom I met while on a Fellowship at Princeton University in 1968, edited some of the earlier drafts and made valuable suggestions which clarified some of my points. Dean Erickson, a former Special Assistant, joined my staff shortly after receiving his MBA from the Massachusetts Institute of Technology. Dean provided analytical skills which gave continuity and objectivity to the book. I owe special thanks to Janice Dessaso, my former secretary at the Commerce Department, who spent many evenings and countless Saturdays and Sundays typing and retyping draft after draft.

Dr. Wilford White, Director of the Small Business Guidance and Development Center at Howard University, provided continuous encouragement. He was also very critical of some of my remarks and thus forced me to strive constantly for excellence.

My wife was most kind and understanding in allowing me to spend most of my evenings during the past four years working on the book. It was only because of her dedication, companionship, and assistance that I was able to complete the book at all.

To Dr. H. Naylor Fitzhugh, my former professor at Howard University and now Vice President of the Pepsi-Cola Company, I dedicate the book. It was because of his constant attention, support, and dedication to his students that I developed a respect for myself and the future of blacks in business.

CONTENTS

INTRODUCTION

The twin facts that both black business and black businessmen were in deep trouble started to become apparent to me the day I graduated from Howard University in 1953. Although I had earned both a Bachelor's and a Master's degree in economics and business administration, I could not find a job that would even remotely take advantage of or compensate me for my educational training. The best that Washington, D.C., the nation's capital, could offer me, in fact, was a choice between being a clerk in the Post Office or a low-ranking apprentice in the National Archives.

And so I decided to go into business for myself. A man or woman should go into business, of course, because he or she sees a need that can be served at a suitable profit. But like so many black people I went into business not because I recognized an opportunity, but because I was desperate to escape from the Establishment. I spent seven of the next ten years going into a succession of small business operations: a door-to-door sales company, a travel agency, a marketing and public relations firm, an auto-repair garage, an auto-brake service, a cosmetics manufacturing firm, a license-renewal service for taxicab drivers, barbers, beauticians, and related activities.

Having just received my academic degrees in economics and business, I assumed that I knew all there was to know about operating a business. I didn't realize —as many others, black and white, don't realize— that a college background doesn't necessarily prepare one for the practical problems of the world of commerce. And because I had neither capital nor access to technical assistance, all of my entrepreneurial endeavors were marginal. I earned a reputation for being a supersalesman, but I did not earn much money. A decade after I graduated from college with so much hope, I reluctantly concluded that under prevailing conditions it was just about impossible for black people to succeed in business except on a mediocre level.

And so in September of 1963 I joined the U.S. Department of Commerce as a junior economist in the Business and Defense Services Administration and I was assigned the task of developing programs that would bring about greater participation of minority people in industry and commerce. When President Nixon created the Office of Minority Business Enterprise on March 5, 1969, I became the agency's first black director and was thus given the job of helping put black and other minority people into business for themselves.

Twenty-one months later, in April of 1971, I decided to leave the federal government. I made the decision primarily because I had become a tired and frustrated warrior in my attempts to change things. Eight years on the front lines of the civil rights movement, trying to move a stubborn, recalcitrant bureaucracy, had taken its toll. I decided to leave, and no sooner had I announced my decision than I was bombarded with requests from the media to give a critique—a "blast" is what I think they had in mind—of the Nixon administration's minority enterprise program. There was some precedent in government for delivering broadside attacks on departure and, as far as I was concerned, there was ample material for such a "critique."

But, as I thought about it, I decided that for several reasons a negative view of black business development would serve no useful purpose. First, any new program, public or private, takes time to organize and get rolling. Second, by creating OMBE the Nixon administration had at least become the first administration ever to recognize by executive order that black people should have roles as the owners and operators of the means of production. Third, I recalled that during the previous ten years I must have read five hundred or more articles on black business development, all criticizing one thing or another. But I could not remember more than two or three articles or books which presented workable plans for resolving the problems of minority business enterprise. Therefore, I could see no benefit or purpose in writing another hot, angry article, which would end up by frustrating the minority community further while adding nothing of real substance to the solution of the problem.

After eighteen years of active involvement in black business enterprise and planning I didn't want my experience to be lost. I wanted to be sure that the people who followed me would not have to reinvent the wheel, to learn painfully, the same way I had learned by stumbling and picking myself up and stumbling again through the years.

Too often the "experts" in black business development ignore what their predecessors have learned, disregard the valuable yield of practical experience. At the very least, therefore, I wanted to leave a record, to write a book that would offer direction to those who would come after me.

At times, particularly in the early chapters of this book, the condition of black business will seem very dim indeed, almost hopeless. It will seem that way because this book approaches black business from the ground-floor level, that is from the perspective of the black businessman himself, who sees no way of getting off the treadmill of drudgery and bare subsistence. But as the book progresses, a mood of optimism evolves as we begin to see that the black businessman is not doomed and that there are solutions, although not easy ones, to his multiple problems.

The truth is that I don't believe that black business is finished, that we might as well post the bankruptcy notices and padlock the doors. The mood of this book is optimistic; the motive is to present ways in which black business can become a vital part of a healthy black community and a lively segment of the national economy. First, I will state the problem in its historical and cultural perspective; then, I will try to dispel some black and white myths about what black business is and what it should be; and finally, in the major portion of this book, I want to spell out ways in which we can begin to resolve the dilemma and begin to perceive what the future might hold.

Clearly, black business development will not cure all the ills of the black community. Black businesses will not, by themselves, transform bleak ghettos into cheerful suburbs nor will they necessarily turn racial fear and hatred into trust and brotherhood. Black businesses will employ some black people, but not nearly all the black people who are unemployed or underemployed. Black businesses will raise the income level of some people, but not of all people. Black businesses will help generate economic and political power, but they will not create a self-sufficient minority community.

Black business development may have no effect whatever on the high rate of crime in the cities or the lack of decent medical care for four-fifths of our population. Nor is black business ownership an end in itself. It is only a means to an end—economic health—along with many other means.

But at the very least it will give the black community leverage in the powerful inner councils. To a large degree the decision makers in our society are those who control wealth. Blacks will never stand a chance of being admitted to this select group until we control wealth. Then, and only then, will black people be able to become a part of that elite group called "the movers and the shakers," who set policy and, to a degree, control the lives of all people. A few blacks have ascended to this level: Henry Parks of Parks Sausage Company in Baltimore, Maryland; John Johnson of Ebony Magazine of Chicago, Illinois; and Berkeley Burrell, president of the National Business League in Washington, D.C. These men, and undoubtedly a few others, can pick up the telephone and get to the President and other national and local leaders with relative ease because of their positions of power that derive from controlling wealth.

Black business development is not a panacea. It is only one response to a variety of urgent needs. But it is an important response. "Real equality," as Republican Senator Edward W. Brooke of Massachusetts put it, "will be impossible if the white race is to be a race of owners and managers and the black race is to be one of employees and laborers."

1   THE THREE-FIFTHS MAN

There is a cruel and ironic theme that threads its way through the history of the black man in America. It's the story of the Three-Fifths Man. When the United States Constitution was ratified in 1789, the Negro was counted as three fifths of a man for purposes of taxation and representation. Now, almost two hundred years later, the black man is counted as a whole man by the census taker and the tax collector, but when the black man comes up before the paymaster, he is still the Three-Fifths Man. The result is as simple and as disheartening as this: the median white family had an income of $9,794 in 1969, the latest year for which complete figures are available. The median black family had an income of only $5,999.[1]

[1] U.S. Department of Labor, Bureau of Labor Statistics, 1971. Bulletin 1699.

Part of the reason that we get short-changed is simply that blacks don't participate in those economic activities which will enable us to earn a sufficient amount of money. For example, 11.1 percent of white workers hold desirable, remunerative jobs as managers, officials and proprietors, while only 2.6 percent of the black and other minority workers hold such positions. At the low end of the scale, blacks hold a disproportionate number of low-paying jobs, those that whites no longer want or never wanted in the first place. Black unemployment chronically runs at twice the rate of white unemployment and some black people are so far down that they have fallen out of the bottom of the labor market altogether, and so are no longer even counted among the unemployed.

Because the focus of this book will be on the black entrepreneur, let's isolate the 2.6 percent of the black labor force which is supposedly in that elite class of proprietors, officials and managers. Let's examine their condition. To begin with, there is no need to consider the troubles of the big black businessman, worried about low morale on the assembly line, stockholder revolts, consumer activism, and environmental legislation. With one or two exceptions, there simply are no big black businessmen.

Black business is almost universally small business and even within small business black businessmen constitute a disadvantaged class. In 1969 the U.S. Census Bureau sought out and tallied up some 163,000 black-owned businesses with total receipts in that year of $4.5 billion, insignificant when compared to a gross national product which at that time was nearing the $1 trillion, that is, the $1,000 billion mark.

Most black businesses are in the service and trade industries, and most black businesses are only marginally successful. If free family labor had to be paid for, many black businesses probably would collapse overnight. Most black businesses are relegated to black neighborhoods, that is, relegated to doing business with only a small percentage of the population. There is not a city in this country where there are more than two or three black-owned businesses in the downtown area, patronized by whites as well as blacks. And even the sheltered black business, an offshoot of segregation, is being threatened. Major downtown department stores, for example, now display black mannequins in their newspaper ads, making it clear that they are willing to accept money from black consumers. The white businessman is signaling that he is interested in selling not just to the white 88 percent of the population but to the entire 100 percent of the population.

Thus, unless some action is taken quickly, black businessmen will never share in the wage and salary gains that black workers have made in the past few years. The black businessman is finding it more and more difficult every day to eke out a living from our 12 percent of the population. And if the current rate of deterioration continues, black business will simply fade away altogether. There are only two alternatives, and the status quo is not one of them. Either black business must grow or it will die.

It is my conviction that black business must not be allowed to die, for if it does, it will mean more than just economic hardship for those 163,000 existing black businesses. It will mean that there will never be big black businesses which will employ significant numbers of black people. But perhaps even more important than that is the crushing blow that it would deliver to our morale and spirit. For now and for the foreseeable future the business of America is going to be business, and if black people do not acquire a proportionate share of American business we are going to drift forever in the backwater of the American economy.

How can black business grow and thrive? The key is in understanding why black business never grew in the first place, why it has always been the stunted child of segregation.

Primarily, the problem of black business can be traced to the fact that for two hundred years, or all through a period of astonishing and ever accelerating growth and refinement, the American business system excluded black people. Black people were cut off not simply from the money and the real estate and the customers but, more fundamentally, separated from that voluminous and still expanding body of knowledge that dictates the way of doing business. Black people were excluded from the business system.

There is no black business system which we can improve and expand. A black business system simply does not exist, although there is a misguided black business folklore which I will discuss in Chapter 3. There is only the white business system, specifically the white American business system. Whatever its spiritual shortcomings, the "American way" has been a spectacularly efficient and productive economic system, envied and emulated not only by poor societies but, somewhat resentfully, by the rich societies of Western Europe, white America's motherland, as well. The system not only exists, it permeates everything in the American economy. All the standards and procedures have been written down, clarified, expanded, formulized, packaged, tested and retested over the years so that everything from borrowing rates to the display of items on the shelf has been worked out in detail.

The system is essential for successful business. Any man, black or white, who goes into business without understanding its procedures and techniques can be saved only by irrepressible genius or divine intervention. And what has happened to the black man is this. The white youngster begins to learn the language and procedures of this system as routinely as he learns to ride a bike. It is part of his everyday environment, the dinner-table conversation, his older brother's accounting textbook, the visit to his uncle's textile plant. Just as routinely, the black youngster is excluded from this experience. It isn't even necessarily part of a conscious effort on the part of the white community to keep this information from him. Business is simply not part of his everyday world and, of course, segregated housing patterns perpetuate his exclusion from this world.

The problem that this book will deal with, therefore, is clear, although far from simple. How do we transmit that body of knowledge, that indispensable package of techniques and procedures to the black businessman so that he will truly have an equal chance at the starting line. Before getting to that problem, however, I want first of all to try to dispel some of the myths about what black business is and what black business should be.

2   MYTHOLOGY

Black business—or at least talking about black business—has become fashionable in corporate board rooms, in government councils, and in news rooms. Black people and white people talk about what black business is and what black business should be. I don't want to debunk either the sincere concern of many whites or the soaring enthusiasm of many blacks. But all too often the talk is out of this world—pure, prime-grade fantasy.

The reasons are understandable. The board members of major corporations are by definition big businessmen who are inclined to think in terms of big projects, even when the black man who will have to run the big project has never had the chance to handle even a small operation. Government bureaucrats respond to political pressure and therefore tend to favor the undertaking that will employ, and therefore quiet, at least temporarily, the largest number of people, even though the venture shakes and wobbles from top to bottom. Newspaper, magazine, and radio and television reporters and editors are enamoured with the unusual and the glamorous. An Afro boutique is more exciting to photograph and more stimulating to write about than a refurbished dry-cleaning plant, even though the boutique is a pipe dream and the dry-cleaning plant is a solid prospect.

A mythology about black business has been promulgated, therefore, by different kinds of people: the well-meaning but misguided white who thinks he knows what's good for the black community; the cynical white who wants to overload the black man with a project he knows can't work and thereby have his prejudices about black incompetence confirmed; the misinformed black who has been given poor direction on what can and what cannot be realistically accomplished; and the opportunistic black who is more interested in a windfall or a get-rich-quick scheme than an undertaking that inevitably will require an enormous amount of energy and patience.

Traveling around the country, I have heard many myths about black business from both black businessmen and white businessmen. Here are some of them, each followed by what I believe is a fair and realistic appraisal.

All you really need to succeed in business is money.

Four ingredients are absolutely necessary for even a fair chance—a qualifiable man, a realistic opportunity, adequate capital, and continuing managerial and technical assistance. Of these four, the man is the most important. He must have entrepreneurial talent, the desire and stamina to succeed, and the willingness to take a risk.

Nonprofit corporations should run black business.

Nonprofit corporations always end up achieving at least one of their objectives: they don't make a profit. The profit motive is the only motive that inspires entrepreneurial achievement.

Cooperatives are the answer to black economic development.

Cooperatives have their place, but they work best in rural areas where a common service is needed and cannot be provided profitably by an entrepreneur. They have not been very successful in urban areas. Poor people with limited funds tend to shop at the nearest location, rather than the centralized cooperative, in order to save time and transportation costs. Also, poor people need credit, which cooperatives do not provide.

I am not interested in making fat cats out of individual blacks.

Why not? The individual entrepreneur is basic to our system. There must be a driving force behind a small business, or it will not succeed. Black capitalism and white capitalism are the same game, and so why should the investor change the rules when black people become involved?

Manufacturing is what you should go into.

Developing and maintaining a market for manufactured goods is a most complex and expensive proposition. If those persons who are encouraging black businessmen to go into manufacturing are sincere, they should first help the existing black manufacturers who are struggling to survive.

Do something big.

This argument, often offered by white businessmen, goes, "If you want my help, you have to think of something big, something worth my time and effort." To these advisers every reasonable project is too small. At the same time, if a black team proposes a million-dollar deal, the white investor replies, "That's too ambitious. Learn to crawl before you walk."

Forget the mom-and-pop operation. It's too small.

This is the corollary to the "think big" argument. The potential white backer discourages the mom-and-pop store, that is, a business run by a man and his wife or son, contending that it will never yield more than mediocre earnings. That's probably true, but in the black community where the majority of people earn less than $8,000 a year, the mom-and-pop store that earns more than $8,000 a year would provide a relatively comfortable living for a man with a family.

The ideology behind black business is militant and separatist.

If an Italian wants to open a store in an Italian

neighborhood or a Pole wants to open a shop in a Polish neighborhood, nobody becomes suspicious about the ideology that's motivating him. It's obvious. He wants to run a business and make a profit. But if a black wants to start a business in a black neighborhood, many whites see it as an aggressive, divisive move, directed not at making a profit but at getting even with white merchants. Whites must learn that black business development will not widen the gap between black and white but will bring them closer together by bringing both the income and the structure of the black community closer in line with that of the white community.

Capitalism—black or white—is exploitative and blacks should stay out it.

While it might be worthwhile to discuss the merits of other political and economic systems, the majority of black people must concentrate on the simpler issue of full participation in the society as it is at this time, and this is a capitalist society. Discouraging blacks from participating in the capitalist system only retards the economic growth of the black community.

Blacks don't want handouts. They want to make it on their own.

I have heard white people state this premise categorically. But why should black people be different? Handouts have become a basic part of the American economy. When they are given to southern senators for not planting crops or to bankrupt aerospace corporations, they are called subsidies or government loans.

When they are given to black people they are called welfare or charity.

Going into business is a civil right.

The development of black business is part of the civil rights movement. But having a business is not a guaranteed, protected individual right for every citizen, such as an education or the vote. It is not simply an extension of equal job opportunity. It requires total commitment and few people—black or white—will ever qualify.

I don't need my own money to go into business. The bank will lend me everything.

There are two types of capital which go into a business. First of all there is the equity capital, the front money, which is usually the entrepreneur's own money or money secured from investors through the sale of stock or long-term bonds. Equity capital generally stays in the business for the entire lifetime of the business and it is equity capital which generates the entrepreneur's profit. Banks do not provide equity capital. Banks make loans which generally have to be paid back within three years. Therefore, the entrepreneur must definitely invest his own money in the business venture.

I didn't get the loan because I'm black.

In an increasing number of cases, loans are denied not because of color but because the would-be entrepreneur is simply not familiar with the procedures and requirements of financial institutions. Thus, attempts to gain the cooperation of financial institutions may have to be directed to the borrower as well as the lender.

The white bank will put up the money.

Because of the low return on investments in most existing black businesses, white investors will be reluctant to put their money in black businesses until a growth trend is established. The black community must direct a major effort to obtain necessary capital from our own churches, Masonic groups, doctors, dentists, attorneys, and others.

Black people will trade with me because I am black.

Black owners will find that their success in attracting customers is inextricably tied to efficiency, competence, and competitiveness. People shop at the place that gives the best dollar value. There is no evidence to support the hope that black consumers will turn automatically to black businessmen for their needs.

You have to have property.

Blacks are too eager for real estate, a carryover from our rural attachment to landholdings. Black people believe that it is mandatory to own a physical plant, while white people want to get rid of theirs and avoid the heavy costs of taxes, insurance, and maintenance. Under such conditions it's easy to see how overly eager black people get stuck with liabilities.

If another black businessman is selling the same thing I am, he is my opponent.

True, you may have to compete with him in some

cases, but you also have to cooperate with him for your mutual benefit. The value of trade associations will be discussed fully in Chapter 4.

I'm doing just fine, keeping my head above water.

Too many black entrepreneurs are level maintainers, content with making just enough money, setting just enough markup to enable them to live in moderate comfort. Black businessmen must be more profit oriented. In this growth-minded economy, a business which does not move ahead, does not really stand still either. It dwindles. Anyhow, what's wrong with getting rich?

A black business must be run entirely by black people.

Pride of black ownership should not be allowed to weaken the business's commitment to profitable operations. If it requires white personnel at various key levels within the operation to make the business profitable, then this need should not be ignored merely for the sake of the claim that the business is totally black owned and operated. Moreover, a "black only" policy would be racism in reverse, which would delay the arrival of the day when blacks and whites can be employers and employees with equal opportunity.

Credit unions should finance business development.

Credit unions are a relatively new means of achieving financial cooperation among black people. As such, they are useful vehicles, but they are not really major vehicles for business development. Like cooperatives, credit unions are primarily organizations to encourage savings, not to provide capital formation. Credit unions function well in churches and other nonprofit entities, but provide little hope as a source of equity capital to entrepreneurs, except on a very limited basis.

Don't tell me about training. Training is a dead end.

Training has become a dirty word in the black community because too often it has been used to perpetuate discriminatory practices. But the truth is, training, the proper kind of training, is essential to black economic development. The trouble with much of the training offered up to now is that it has been job-oriented and that many of the programs have led either to low-level positions with limited futures or have failed entirely to follow through with actual job opportunities for trainees. It will require skill, therefore, to develop training programs that can inspire or motivate the participation of prospective trainees. This can be accomplished if promotional emphasis is placed upon operational techniques as opposed to academic or philosophical theorizing.

Another reason that training has received such a bad name is the great shortage of instructors, of trained personnel who can effectively supervise or take staff positions in business development organizations. We must somehow train the trainers, because a lack of sensitive persons who understand the techniques of business has contributed substantially to the ineffectiveness of many programs. Training must be provided at all levels to prospective entrepreneurs and operators of existing marginal firms. Some training funds are available through the Manpower Development and

Training Act and On the Job Training Program, but because these programs are primarily aimed at employment, it will take imaginative, well-conceived proposals to divert the substantial funds needed for entrepreneurial training.

Black people can do better in the professions than in business.

Bright young blacks have traditionally gone into the professions—teaching, medicine, law, the ministry—because the professions offered high income and a chance to help the brothers. But the income figures gathered by Andrew Brimmer, the black governor of the Federal Reserve Board, show that per year of education blacks actually earn more money in business than in the professions.[1] And young blacks whose main desire is to build their own community can do nothing more valuable than help provide the community with economic vitality. It is especially important that measures be taken to instill this community pride and desire to go into business in young black college and business school graduates who are presently being actively and successfully recruited by large white corporations. In addition, efforts should be made to motivate those individuals who are already at work in large corporations so that they can lend their practical knowledge to the struggle for black business development.

[1] Andrew Brimmer, "The Negro in the National Economy," in the "American Negro Reference Book," ed. by John P. Davis (Englewood Cliffs, N.J.: Prentice-Hall, Inc., 1966), p. 296.

Mythical answers to the dilemmas of black business-men form a cloud of confusion which chokes the spirit of the aspiring black entrepreneur. It relegates him to a life of mediocrity. I can remember so well when I finished college and left the ghetto to face the white world for the first time. I almost believed many of the myths. By the time white folks, as well as black folks who had lost hope, told me for the fifteenth time that I was going to be a failure, they almost had me believing it. A black person who hears a myth over and over again begins to accept it himself, begins to accept the myth that he has no power to change the situation even though he is determined to work hard. I guess that it goes back to the old saying, "As you think, so shall you be."

It is crucial that blacks in this day and age do not allow mythical answers to kill their spirit and as a result develop misshapen ideas about what's right and what's wrong for black folks to do, about what the requirements are for successful entrepreneurs. So much for the mythical answers to the problems of black business. In the following chapters the real answers will be presented and explained.

3   SYSTEMS AND PROCEDURES

My grandfather was an entrepreneur, a persistent entrepreneur. Until some unknown persons burned his place down because he was "uppity," he owned a funeral home in Virginia. But even the fire couldn't burn out his spirit. He stayed an entrepreneur, and I can remember that throughout my early life my grandfather was always buying and selling. He would buy apples for one cent at the wholesale market and then retail them for two cents. That was the way business was transacted, he told me: Buy it for one cent and sell it for two.

Grandfather, unfortunately, was wrong. He was wrong not because of his stamina and his eagerness for profit. These were sound entrepreneurial instincts. He was wrong because he should have been charging 1.7

cents for those apples or maybe 2.3 cents, or whatever price made sense in terms of his costs and factors of competitive position. The point is that my grandfather had no idea what to charge. Apparently, he had overheard someone say at one time or another that you should mark up your price 50 percent or 100 percent. My grandfather never knew that there are definite procedures and forces in the market place which determine the price of fruit and vegetables as well as everything else. He went into one business after another without understanding the system that governed that business and that invariably would determine whether or not the business would be successful.

More unfortunately, I carried out the tradition. I went into the travel business with no experience or without even having talked to anyone who had run a travel agency. I tried to do it all on my own, based on what I now call an "ignorance syndrome." I didn't even know that it was possible to buy rooms overseas on a wholesale basis. I was making plans for a group that was going to Europe and I didn't know that there was an office in New York that I could have wired to get a quote on the price of the rooms. An accountant, who had never worked in a travel agency before, and I struggled with an inadequate bookkeeping system. Eventually, a friend at Northwest Airlines told me that the entire system for getting rooms and booking tours as well as everything else worth knowing about the travel business had already been worked out as a step-by-step procedure and that there was even a bookkeeping system that could be installed immediately. But it was too late. I had already lost my $25,000 and was out of business.

Most unfortunate of all, the heritage that was passed from my grandfather to me was not unusual. It was the typical heritage of the black community, a heritage that leads to a cycle of failure and frustration. In fact, black business today is, in most cases, practically synonymous with frustration and failure.

Black people have been engaged in American business almost as long as we have been in America, but always in unattractive roles. True, some freed men and escaped slaves owned taverns and barber shops and livery stables well before Emancipation, but the typical black man in business clearly had the subservient role, a role that was barely distinguishable from plantation labor. If there was an opening for one salesclerk, frequently two men would be given the job, one white and one black. The black man would do the manual labor, such as carrying the flour sacks in from the storeroom, and the white man would do the sales job and collect the money from the customer. The system had at least two deleterious effects. The black man was deprived of the experience of handling sales transactions and money, and to the black community business came to mean not selling and profit making but sweeping and sack hauling.

And even the relatively few successful black business communities were overwhelmed by the waves of European migration of the late nineteenth century.

Back in 1847, for example, Philadelphia was a city of only 340,000. The black population could not have been much more than 10 percent of the total, because at the time there were only 53,000 black people in the entire state of Pennsylvania. Still, the tiny black business community of Philadelphia must have had a look of at least modest prosperity about it. In addition to some five hundred mechanics, it included successful caterers, a sail manufacturer, a broker, a lumber merchant, and several investors who were acquiring wealth in railroad stock, the meat business, and real estate.[1]

According to the 1970 census there are now 635,-791 black people in the City of Brotherly Love out of a total population of 1,950,098. But despite that huge population growth a survey conducted several years ago indicates that, if anything, the black business community has declined. Most of the black businesses are now in the service and retail trades and are very small. They compare in size with many white businesses as they were thirty, forty, or even fifty years ago and are conducted at low levels of efficiency and profitability. Here is what the survey showed:[2]

[1] "The Negro as a Businessman," J. H. Harmon Jr., Arnett G. Lindsay, and Carter G. Woodson (College Park, Md.: McGrath Publishing Co., 1969, © 1929), p. 5.

[2] Drexel Institute of Technology, "An Analysis of the Little Businessman in Philadelphia," and "The Census of Negro Owned Businesses" (Philadelphia: Drexel Institute of Technology, 1964). Information from the Drexel study is presented here as it was summarized in Eugene Foley's article, "The Negro Businessman: In Search of a Tradition," in "The Negro American," Talcott Parsons and Kenneth Clark, eds. (Boston: Houghton Mifflin Company, 1966), pp. 560–563.

27

Blacks operated only thirteen manufacturing concerns, all small:

8 beauty products manufacturing companies
1 casket manufacturing company
2 clothing manufacturing companies
1 ironworks manufacturing company
1 meat company

Blacks operated only fourteen wholesale distribution companies:

8 beauty products
1 casket
1 candy, notions and novelties
1 clothing
3 food

While about ten black-owned businesses—insurance, publishing, catering, cosmetic supplies, and contracting—were quite successful, most of the 4,242 black businesses were marginal in profit-making ability, stability, and physical condition. Most were sole proprietorships and many would be submarginal if free family labor were not available. For example, median **sales** were:

$2,500 for black-owned beauty shops
4,400 for black-owned barber shops
6,800 for black-owned luncheonettes

Almost all black businesses were located in primarily black neighborhoods, but at least half of the businesses in those neighborhoods were white-owned.

The study rated the general appearance of each business; of the black establishments in the largest black community business area:

12.1 percent were "neat and clean"
55.9 percent were "not eye-appealing"
32.0 percent were "rundown"

The nearly one-third that were described as "rundown" had "paint peeling off walls, plaster coming off ceilings, little or no lighting, no displays to speak of, and little stock on hand."

Black business in Philadelphia is more or less representative of black business everywhere, and everywhere one generation of dreary subsistence simply encourages another generation of the same. In the white community businessmen are generally community leaders, who influence not only the economy but the community's social and political activities as well. But black businessmen, struggling to survive, have neither the time nor the stature to serve as community leaders. Thus, the neighborhood and the community at large are deprived of what could and should be one of their strongest stabilizing influences and inspirations, the leadership of black businessmen who have an important stake in the future of the community.

The black businessman realizes that in the eyes of the community he is a symbol of frustration and hopelessness, rather than an example of achievement, success, and leadership. His own self-image declines even further. In the end, business is not a polite word in the black community, and black parents generally discourage their children from pursuing business careers, either as executives or as entrepreneurs.

No reservoir of business knowledge and heritage accumulates in the black community and so each new black entrepreneur starts out from scratch and develops what little expertise he can through trial and error. Things would be difficult enough for him under the best of circumstances but when he has to compete against a white businessman who has already assimilated the systems and procedures, the results for the black businessman are disastrous.

Consider the case of several black dry-cleaning shops in Washington, D.C., several years ago. They were charging $1.10 to clean and press a suit until they learned that a large white-owned chain was charging only 69 cents a suit. To be competitive the black operators dropped their price as well. But what they didn't realize was that the large chain had one machine that could clean several hundred suits at a time. That reduced the chain's cost factor to 20 cents a suit because the machine was operating at full capacity. The individual black operators had machines that could clean only a hundred suits at a time, and so their cost factors were 50 cents a suit, two and one half times as much as that of the chain. The black entrepreneurs did not understand economies of scale. They did not understand that pricing is based not only on what the competition is charging but on costs—the cost of raw materials, the cost of labor, overhead, and interest on loans. There is a clear and indispensable formula that must be followed.

To go into business without understanding the systems, procedures, and techniques by which that business is run would be suicidal and in most cases it has been a suicidal effort for black entrepreneurs. The techniques govern every aspect of business—financing, accounting, hiring, advertising, merchandising—down to the smallest detail. When I first graduated from Howard University I took part in a research project for Coca-Cola in which I did nothing but observe which hand supermarket customers used to open the doors of soft-drink coolers. The study concluded that most people opened the door with their right hands and their bodies were therefore in such a position that they could look and reach most easily into the left hand side of the locker. Not surprisingly, Coca-Cola executives set out to have their bottles placed on the left side of the coolers. To run a supermarket without understanding customer behavior is a serious handicap. To compete with Coca-Cola without understanding customer behavior is madness.

The white businessman, as I pointed out earlier, begins to learn these techniques, or at least the theories on which they are based, from a very early age. How do we transmit these systems and procedures, the way of doing things, to black people so that we interrupt and destroy our cycle of frustration and failure. It would be impractical for the black business community to start back where the white business community was two hundred years ago and try to catch up by imitating the two-century-long development that the white business community went through. It does not make sense for the black business community to learn by progressing by trial and error, piece of information piled laboriously on piece of information over the years, from the small store to the tiny group of stores to the great chain. Because the systems and procedures of the white community are still growing, the black business community simply would never catch up. Besides, it does not make good business sense to do work that has already been done. That is certainly one basic procedure itself.

What we need therefore are ways and means of intercepting and learning the systems and procedures as they are now, of tapping that accumulated body of techniques as it develops. Fortunately, there already are in existence institutions which can be adapted to this purpose, which can become tools of development for the black businessman.

These programmatic designs will be directed in two areas: programs to improve the efficiency and profitability of business presently owned by blacks; and programs designed to encourage a greater entrepreneurial interest on the part of black people so that new black businesses can be established.

4   STRENGTH IN NUMBERS

The black businessman is the forgotten man of contemporary capitalism, fifty to a hundred years behind the times in the systems and procedures that he uses. In most instances, he barely makes enough money to survive. He is weak and he is lonely. He can't even cash in very effectively on the current rash of attention given to black business by the press, the government, the corporation, and the black community itself because they are generally more interested in the new black business, the black business to be, than they are in the ramshackle black business that has been struggling to survive. About the only thing that the black businessman has going for him is the sure knowledge that there are many, many others in the same predicament. And that is a clue to one solution of his dilemma. By himself the black businessman is all but powerless, but in union with many other black businessmen he can be strong.

The concept of the businessman's union has existed in the white community at least since the Middle Ages when trade and craftsmen banded together in guilds. Today white businessmen are linked together in numerous overlapping and interlocking organizations, such as Rotaries and chambers of commerce. Perhaps one of the most effective organizations is the trade association, an organization of successful businessmen having similar interests and needs who can benefit from cooperative effort. Working together allows them to retain their individual pride and freedom while discovering, through action and involvement, the merit of cooperation and mutual improvement. Together they can achieve economies of scale in purchasing, group advertising, employee benefits, and business services. Among themselves they can exchange information on quality standards, pricing policies, diversification opportunities, and operating techniques.

The existing trade association would, in fact, be an ideal structure for "bootstrap"—upgrading of black businesses—except for one important requirement: the trade association is an amalgamation for established firms that are at least moderately successful. Most existing black firms are not successful according to the standards of the white business community. Indeed, by a strict definition of "business" many black firms are not really businesses at all but simply self-employed individuals who get paid for labor but do not make a profit of any kind. In addition they are very small and, in most cases, are not operated according to proper business systems and procedures. Most black businesses would be excluded from trade associations today simply because they are not on a par with successful businesses.

Thus, black entrepreneurs need something that is similar in structure to a trade association but radically different in level of emphasis. The black structure must do more than offer economies in purchasing, advertising, and so forth. It must stress education in business systems and procedures. The point may seem trivial but actual experience has shown that education and the establishment of procedures and systems is the most vital service needed by a majority of black businessmen. For that reason the structure that I am suggesting as an initial step is one I would call not a trade association but a business organization.

A "business organization" can be defined as the cooperative joining of businesses engaged in similar or identical lines of business activity into a trade association—through which a standardization of operational procedures and marketing techniques is initiated. This allows the individual participating firms an opportunity to upgrade themselves in order to meet the minimal operational standards and requirements for survival and growth in the general market—the total effort being directed at maximizing efficiency and profitability. Changes and variations in the basic formula are made, of course, when it is necessary to resolve specific problems of minority-group persons. This concept ties in the key elements and ingredients reflected in the evolution of capitalism—from the mom-and-pop store to the voluntary chain, to the large corporation, and finally to the commercial or industrial giant.

The business organization concept is a tested and proved mechanism. As a model and as an illustration of the depth of assistance that is needed, consider the following experience:

The first experiment to test the feasibility of the business organization concept among black businessmen was conceived by my former staff at the U.S. Department of Commerce in early 1964. The experiment was conducted by Howard University in Washington, D.C., through its Small Business Guidance and Development Center. This project, entitled "Local Economic Organization," was funded in July 1966 by the Economic Development Administration of the U.S. Department of Commerce. Minority dry-cleaners were selected as the group to be organized; there were approximately 125 black shop owners in the District of Columbia. Through an analysis of these shops, their problems were classified in the following categories:

Quality controls. Many shops were not adhering to strict quality standards, garments too often were smelling heavily of solvent, dye synthesizers were seldom used to prevent bleeding, "sizing" was not always used to give garments body, and too many garments were being put in a single bag, etc.

Physical appearance. Many shops were unattractive to potential customers. Outside signs were not always properly lettered or lighted. Windows were often dirty and displays were antiquated or nonexistent in many stores. Counters were poorly constructed and quite often the wrong size. Price lists were either poorly lettered or not available. The interior decor was almost always in poor taste and the garments were not maintained or presented to customers in the most appealing manner.

Customer services. Many shops were handling only drycleaning and missing profits on related services such as hat blocking, shoe repair, shirt laundering, etc.

Accounting systems. Most shops lacked efficient bookkeeping systems and thus were unable to determine costs and profits.

Employee benefits. Most shops had no group hospitalization programs or retirement plans and thus were unable to keep good employees.

Purchasing. Most shops were paying higher prices for supplies due to purchases in small quantity.

It should be made clear that there were a number of black shops which did adhere to strict controls in all areas. These obviously were the more profitable shops. However, they were the exception rather than the rule.

Once the industry analysis had been completed, the action phase of the program was initiated. Three staff persons were hired by the university to carry out the project: a staff director, a field representative, and a secretary.

The vehicle selected for organizing the shop owners was the Capital Dry Cleaners Association (CDA), officially formed February 14, 1966. This was accomplished by calling a meeting of the shop owners to discuss "a program conducted by Howard University and the U.S. Department of Commerce to assist dry-cleaners in improving the efficiency and profitability of their business." A letter and personal visits were necessary to generate interest and allay initial doubts and fears. Once the trade association was organized, a standardization of operational procedures was initiated:

Quality controls. With the assistance of the Neighborhood Cleaners Association of New York City and the National Institute of Dry Cleaners in Silver Spring, Maryland, a set of quality standards was developed and a program of adherence of these standards was instituted to insure that quality and workmanship met normal commercial standards.

Image control. Minimal standards for the physical appearance of member stores were developed and checked against the actual image projected by member stores. (An architect should be used to carry out this function in the future.)

Training. A program to upgrade counter-girl skills and entrepreneurial skills of shop owners was implemented. Counter girls were taken into a classroom setting where they discussed the more obvious facets of a successful business operation. Many of these young women realized for the first time that the store in which they worked might very well fail or succeed based on their ability to attract and handle customers.

Shop owners were given similar instructions, but in more detail. Special emphasis was placed on operational efficiency:

Accounting. A standardized accounting system, representing the most efficient system for a dry-cleaner, was made available to member shops and installed, where possible, by two accountants.

Group purchasing. Some group purchasing of hangers and garment bags with the CDA insignia was undertaken with substantial saving to individual shop owners.

Group insurance. A group insurance plan offering life insurance was made available—with tremendous savings made possible because of the large number of participants.

Credit union. A credit union was organized for the benefit of the membership.

Services. Customer services such as shirt laundry and shoe repair, previously not offered by some shops, were made available through wholesalers or other member shops with idle capacity.

Offices. The Association eventually purchased a building to be used for executive offices, meeting place, group purchasing warehouse, credit union office, secretarial service center, and an employment center.

Because membership fees and dues had to be kept

at a minimum, the building and other Association expenses not covered by the CDA funding were paid from the profits accumulated by the Association through its mass purchasing operation.

Employment. Since the inception of the project many member shops have added new employees and opened new outlets as a result of their affiliation with the Association.

A key ingredient in the Howard experiment was the cooperation of the National Institute of Dry Cleaners and the Neighborhood Cleaners Association. Their expertise and guidance made the design and implementation of standardized operational procedures and marketing techniques relatively easy.

One might ask why the typical mainstream trade association would want to help develop more viable business in its industry. Isn't that creating more competition? The answer is NO. First, any businessman gets a significant boost in his ego from passing on the lessons he has learned; he is usually very happy to be a bridge builder for those who have a sincere desire to follow in his footsteps. Second, such assistance is really motivated by enlightened self-interest. Trade associations want as many members as possible to line their association treasury and help build their collective strength. In most cases, they don't turn away black businessmen because of racist discrimination, but simply because they know that the average black firm has nothing to contribute. By bringing black firms to a level of viable profitability they are creating more potential members for the cause. Black business organizations such as the Capital Dry Cleaners won't remain on the sidelines forever; they will eventually merge into the mainstream trade association; another example of black business development as a move toward integration. This project experienced many problems and represented only a beginning. A lot of work remains to be done before this process can be perfected. However, we must start somewhere and we must start now.

The lesson for business-development groups should be clear: initiation of business organization associations is a very effective way of helping existing minority businessmen to help themselves. The model could be applied to nearly any "industry" in any city. In fact, the business-organization concept has the advantage of being horizontally expandable. From the dry-cleaners, a local business development group could move to the contractors, the restaurateurs, the manufacturers, and so on without limit.

Let's consider some other opportunities which might be aided by the business-organization concept in Washington, D.C. There are approximately 327 black-owned beauty shops and 220 black-owned barber shops that together spend over $1.6 million each year for the goods and services needed to operate their businesses. That includes cosmetics, hair preparations, soaps, janitorial supplies, linen rentals, window-cleaning services, accounting and tax services, and many others.

If those 547 shops would form a corporation to sell themselves the goods and services that they are now buying from a hundred different places, it is likely that the corporation could make a gross profit of 25 percent a year or approximately $400,000 from the sale of the same goods and services that are now being purchased elsewhere. As the operators gained experience and became more efficient, they might bring in even greater profits, profits that might be used to establish a group hospitalization plan, a retirement program, training courses, computerized accounting, legal services—all the things those black businessmen can't afford now.

Also in Washington there are approximately ten black fuel oil distributors who each buy about 1.5 million gallons or more of oil every year. That volume is not very significant in the market place. But a 15-million-gallon dealer is significant. If the ten black distributors could combine their requirements and negotiate as a wholesaler, they could buy their fuel oil for approximately 25 percent less, thus saving about $400,000 a year.

Similar opportunities undoubtedly exist among Washington's 47 black automobile shops, 36 black convalescent homes, 42 black day nurseries, 146 black dry-cleaners, 23 black employment services, 14 florist shops, 44 funeral directors, 42 radio and television service and sales shops, 31 shoe repair shops, 48 tourist homes, 58 carry-out shops, 34 delicatessens, 22 drug stores, 56 grocery stores, 10 liquor stores, 43 restaurants, 48 restaurant/bars, 101 service stations, 20 variety stores, 79 building and home improvement firms, 16 painting, paper hanging, and plastering establishments, 27 taxicab associations, 27 transfer and storage houses, 23 trucking and hauling firms, 73 real estate offices, and 17 print shops.

After each one of these separate classifications of business organize horizontally, the next step is to organize them vertically, that is, the business organization from each industry would join a total community business organization. The potentials are truly impressive. Over a ten-year period, for example, the beauty shops and barber shops would have raised their gross profits by approximately $4 million through joint purchasing alone. The fuel oil distributors would have done the same. Admittedly this evaluation is optimistic, but what if the 23 other categories of business in Washington could increase their profits as much? In ten years the black business community in Washington could conceivably increase its profits by $100 million. The total benefit to the community would be tremendous.

The community business organization could offer many of the same advantages of the individual business organization, including group insurance, advertising, and promotional campaigns. But it can do even more than that. It can transcend its maker and become an organization powerful enough to encourage if not demand the cooperation of key bankers and the local government.

If there are a hundred black business communities with the same potential as Washington, then regional organizations and eventually a National Business League have the potential of raising up to $1 billion over a decade. That $1 billion reinvested back in the black community would be an enormous boost. The limits are only those of imagination and organizational effort because the basic concept is a sound, bottoms-up approach based on a realistic appraisal of the problems and potentials of existing minority businessmen.

5   THE FRANCHISE

Statistics have proved that most people lack at least two basic essentials for starting a successful business: adequate financial resources and business and managerial experience. It is ironic that most would-be businessmen, black and white, do not realize their deficiencies!

Each year, thousands of persons confident of their trade skills, yet ignorant of the complex entrepreneurial problems that await them, plunge into self-employment; and each year seven out of each ten go bankrupt, two struggle along as living failures, and one makes it. According to Dun & Bradstreet figures, the chances are only one out of ten that a new enterprise will last eighteen months; even after that, survival for ten years is a five-to-one long shot.

With that pessimistic view of the facts, how can we even talk about starting new black businesses? How can we in good conscience set up sincerely hopeful black entrepreneurs if they stand every chance of getting mowed down by the frightful efficiency of the business establishment?

The answer is, we can't. Morality aside, today's fragile detente between the races just cannot tolerate another batch of promises that don't stand a chance of fulfillment.

Instead, we must find ways to move more aggressively not despite the chance of failure, but **without** it; we can't put every small businessman in a womb of subsidies, but we can put them into packaged business situations that include an already proven set of successful ingredients.

Such a mechanism is the franchise business. Franchising may be described as an arrangement whereby an organization (the franchiser) which has developed a successful retail product or service extends (sells) to individuals (the franchisees) the right and opportunity to engage in business, provided they follow an established pattern of operation. In my opinion, franchising has the potential to provide a sound basis upon which blacks can start new businesses. Under most forms of the system, the franchiser provides managerial training and assistance on a continuing basis, finances equipment, co-signs bank notes, arranges leases for property and sources for equity capital, and helps establish relations with the SBA, local banks and private investors. In addition, franchisers often provide for assistance on location, advertising and merchandising, and give the advantage of centralized purchasing with possible savings. These are things that fill the vital needs of any small business, but one additional factor makes franchising especially attractive for black businesses: the franchise prescribes and enforces strict use of business systems and procedures. Thus, franchising can fulfill the dual function of increasing the number of viable business opportunities at the same time that it is developing among minority groups the essential skills which are the basis for a truly competitive position in business.

Before franchising begins to sound like God's gift to the business world, a cautionary note should be sounded. Not all franchise chains are, in fact, purveyors of successful formulas; further, to the embarrassment of the very professional and sincere franchising firms, some sloppy organizations of rather questionable ethics have moved into this field. Second, as the franchising concept proves more and more successful, many new firms are entering the most common franchise fields (fast-service food, laundromats, etc.), and the duplication and competition is becoming fierce.

But in spite of these and many other problems which are inherent in franchising, I am still convinced that it represents a potentially excellent vehicle for black business development. I say "potentially" excellent because before franchising companies can begin to enlist substantial numbers of black entrepreneurs, they must make two significant modifications in their system.

First, most franchise arrangements require a relatively large initial investment; while much of that initial amount can be financed through conventional bank loans, there usually remains an amount of equity or "front" money that is expected to come from the franchisee. As we have seen, the typical black would-be businessman does not have, for instance, the $100,000 needed to start a fast-service hamburger outlet; even if the amount were only $10,000, it would be very difficult or even impossible for most blacks to raise.

Thus, the franchisers who want to help develop more black ownership in their chains must find a way to soften their entry requirements before they can realistically expect their offers to be attractive to the black businessman. One way to do this would be simply to set aside a block of internal funds that would be reserved for financing the entry of black entrepreneurs; each franchise financed under such a plan would pay back in, say, five equal annual installments, or better, in a certain proportion of his profits until the amount was covered.

The franchisers that have truly successful chains will not find this plan burdensome, since each new outlet should be profitable enough to return the investment shortly; on the other hand, the less successful and less reputable firms, knowing the real expected-earnings outlook for their franchise, will not be willing to take the risk.

The second requirement is this: Most of the better franchisers offer very complete and polished franchisee training courses and continuing management assistance programs. While they are rightfully proud of these training courses, they will find that such programs will have to be amended in some cases to make them suitable for the black entrepreneur. As I have stressed above, the typical black would-be businessman, because he has been excluded in the past, is totally unfamiliar with the simple systems and procedures of the business world; his starting point, the body of expertise that he carries into initial training, in many cases, will be much lower than that of the average franchisee and he will have to be brought up to par by a supplementary sort of "Headstart" initiation course. Afterward, significantly closer attention will have to be paid to his operation on a continuing basis. Again, it is not unfair that the franchisee be required to pay part of the cost as long as it is truly helpful.

Given these two extra measures, the better franchise systems can offer a significant mechanism for creating new black-owned businesses.

With that objective in mind, the U.S. Commerce Department recently compiled and published the "Franchise Company Data Book." This publication identifies franchise firms which do not discriminate on the basis of race, color, religion, or national origin in the availability, terms, or conditions of their franchises; such companies are listed with a description of their operation, present number of franchises, years in operation, equity and other initial capital needed, financial assistance available, training provided, and managerial assistance available.

In the most recent edition, 253 franchisers are listed. The **Franchise Company Data Book** is made available free of charge to the public; approximately 60,000 copies have been distributed. While companies listed are not officially endorsed by the Commerce Department, the book is the only comprehensive list of franchise opportunities for members of minority groups.

Given the many advantages of the franchise plan and the availability of information about franchise opportunities, why have so few blacks opened franchise businesses? Through their efforts to promote franchises among blacks, the Commerce Department and many franchisers themselves have discovered a troublesome credibility gap; not only are many blacks skeptical of business in general, as pointed out above, but most firmly believe that franchising is another "exploitative scheme." At worse, the militant attitude holds that franchises are just another drain on the ghetto economy, a method whereby profits can be siphoned from the community. Presumably these objections could be partially assuaged by black ownership of the more reputable franchise firms, but there is a widespread "belief" in the black community that many franchisers are discriminators, that they bar the black man from ownership through higher fees, larger down payments, poor locations, or poor counseling. Unfortunately, I am told that there is considerable evidence to lead one to this conclusion!

THE DELIVERY MECHANISM

To overcome these negative attitudes against the franchise concept, more than a simple catalogue of opportunities will be needed. The franchisers will have to adopt an aggressive and thorough approach to black business development, but their efforts will have to be coupled with a credible and aggressive delivery mechanism at the community level. As an example of one vehicle that might act independently or in conjunction with community business development groups, I would suggest what might be called the Franchise Business Opportunity Center.

The basic purpose of such a center would be to present franchising in a new light from within a local community setting. It would say to the black community that the franchise industry is not playing games, that it is dead serious about recruiting black prospects.

The Franchise Business Opportunity Center might initially be established as a national vehicle with branch operations in local communities, or it might be established solely as a local vehicle. In essence, the Center would perform the following functions:

It would distribute, along with other business literature, copies of the Commerce Department's "Franchise Company Data Book" to provide for interested persons a comprehensive list of franchise business opportunities with the added assurance that discrimination is not a deterring factor.

It would maintain an active folder on all current franchisers listed in the "Franchise Company Data Book," along with other ethical franchisers qualifying to participate in the program. The folder would include brochures, sample contracts, and all pertinent information regarding the particular franchiser's package. In addition, it would try to have on file signed pledges as concrete evidence of the nondiscriminatory policy of participating franchisers.

The Center would also maintain a library and reference list of all current and significant publications, including articles and books pertaining to the franchise industry in order to provide information and education to potential franchisees and franchisers.

The Center would conduct regular weekly seminars on all phases of franchising. On one level, these seminars would feature visual aids, literature, and case histories designed to enlighten and inspire interested persons and to help them intelligently evaluate franchise opportunities. On another level, the seminars could outline the specific procedures involved in becoming a franchisee and the general day-to-day responsibilities of a franchise businessman.

At the same time, the Center would conduct interviews, aptitude tests, and similar screening devices to determine the suitability and eligibility of prospective franchisees. By applying the criteria and guidelines of various franchisers, the Center could then identify good prospects and put them in contact with the most appropriate companies.

The Center would establish and maintain liaison with local financial institutions such as banks, private investors, SBA offices, MESBICs, and other financial sources to assure that proper financing is available to minority group members and others having entrepreneurial interest.

Employing the business organization concept, the Center might then follow up by organizing and coordinating a minimum of four industry-oriented (e.g., dry-cleaning, food, auto repair, etc.) franchise workshops for local businessmen. By including displays featuring the latest equipment and techniques for improving efficiency and profitability, the workshops would have an additional interest and benefit to those businessmen presently not involved in a franchise network but interested in improving their existing operations.

The Center would constantly seek and coordinate the support of local leaders and organizations to assure full utilization of each and every available resource having a relevance to franchising and the motivation of individual enterprise.

Finally, and perhaps most important, the Center would do everything it could to make sure that prospective franchisees "investigate before they invest." Although the principle of franchising is sound and most franchisers are honest, it is still possible for a man to "dig his own grave" by signing up with a questionable franchiser or getting deeply involved without a full understanding of the business. The Center would improve the franchisee's chance for success by encouraging him to examine each opportunity thoroughly and having his contract analyzed and explained by a competent lawyer.

Ideally, a Center should have a regional responsibility so as to gain maximum coverage of all surrounding areas. This might be achieved by use of a mobile Franchise Center, a used trailer, for instance, that might be furnished and arranged to handle Center services such as seminars, meetings, franchise library material, visual aids, and career counseling. Mobility would be very important in that it would allow coverage with visibility.

EMPLOYMENT AND YOUNG ENTREPRENEURS

One extra benefit of franchise development, of course, would be employment of area residents; in the case of ghetto franchises, these might very well be hitherto hard-core unemployed people. It is the somewhat unusual characteristic of many franchises, notably the fast-service food shops, that they usually employ a number of boys and girls of high school age— precisely the group that presently experiences the highest unemployment rate in the country. Moreover, the highly structured environment of a franchise operation often makes it possible for aggressive teens (or others with low work experience) to function in positions of meaningful responsibility—as night managers, for instance.

Because of the unique operational structure of some franchises, they would be ideal for a "feeder program" —a "learn and earn" course designed to train black youngsters and others in basic business skills and techniques. With the Junior Achievement program in mind, this feeder program might be formalized under a name such as Young Entrepreneurs, Inc.

Young Entrepreneurs, Inc., would be organized to own and operate franchised businesses in urban areas functioning primarily as training vehicles; the number of businesses operated would depend on available resources and possible locations for specific types of businesses. Any person belonging to a minority, between the ages of sixteen and thirty, would be eligible, although high school diplomas might be required or arrangements could be made to incorporate the experience into a work-study program; such a selection requirement would encourage interested dropouts to return to school, at least on the work-study plan. The number of trainees selected would depend on the number needed to operate the unit and the feasible demand that could be made on school time, but an average of thirty to forty full- and part-time workers per unit does not seem impossible—nor insignificant!

To give the youth program real academic meaning and make it more stimulating than "just another job," a somewhat structured training program would be included. The following is a possible format designed specifically for the youth program; many of its features are necessities even for the adult franchisee, however, since he often has no more business experience than a high school student.

FRANCHISE TRAINING

The training format must vary with the specific franchise, of course, but in every case the major emphasis should be on learning through doing, rather than by simple imitation or detailed written instruction.

While most franchise training programs are directed solely at on-the-job training, the youth program should emphasize equally classroom instruction and on-the-job training, including business concepts, academic case studies, and visits to other successful business enterprises. If necessary, a part of the training could be provided through a local adult education facility.

The academic approaches or classroom instruction should be handled in simple, practical language. Included in the curriculum, among other things, might be the following subjects and activities:

Types of business ownership. Sole proprietorship, partnership, corporations; how these relate to the capitalistic system; government controls and their relevance to small business.

Getting along with people. Kinds of people (introverts and extroverts); classes of people (customers, employees, suppliers, government officials, franchisers);

motivation; learning to speak, debate, and write effectively.

Learning about business. Production and distribution, land, labor, capital, and management; the profit system; dynamics of management; kinds of business organization and advantages and disadvantages of each.
Business Operation. Administration v. operation; policies v. practices; management functions, i.e., production, marketing, financing, credit, storage, transportation, housekeeping; case studies involving these functions and general decision making.
Special kinds of business operations. Conventional proprietorship, voluntary chain, cooperative chain, trade associations, franchises; the strengths and weaknesses of each as they operate in the United States.
Field trips. Visiting small and larger businesses in varied trades and industries; preparing analytical reports on visits, and discussing each report.

The most useful academic mix is really a matter of choice, but the total training program should be geared to the most practical application of business principles, designed to produce an individual capable of operating a small business successfully.

Many training programs fail because they do not have well-defined placement procedures for trainee graduates. A number of opportunities should be utilized as "outlets" for Young Entrepreneurs; here are some possibilities:

New franchise businesses would be the primary

prospect, especially for the more mature and financially stable trainees who want to start their own business immediately.

Existing franchise businesses, those participating in the project and a host of others, would be prime prospects for employment.

Small business operators who generally find it difficult to recruit and train employees would provide a wide range of opportunities. Black firms especially could benefit from this pool of trained and "indoctrinated" young people.

The National Business League, Interracial Council for Business Opportunity, National Urban League Skills Bank, and University Small Business Development Centers all over the country could refer Young Entrepreneur graduates to their clients and associate business firms.

THE FUTURE THROUGH FRANCHISING

Young Entrepreneurs, Inc., shows immediately that the concept of franchising can be expanded and modified to go much further than just creation of individual black businesses. And Young Entrepreneurs is just one possibility.

Like the business organization concept, the franchising concept is almost infinitely expandable. It could be extremely helpful to existing black businessmen who have developed a successful product or service or marketing technique. With the help and advice of an energetic promoter, many of them could package their successful system and replicate it in other parts of the city, state, or nation.

Or, several black firms in the same field could turn themselves into a "ready-made franchise network" just by adopting a standardized name and appearance—with all the benefits of a business organization type of amalgamation plus enhanced market appeal. However, I would offer a strong word of caution to the do-something-quick guys. Developing a successful franchise firm is an exceedingly difficult task which should be studied very carefully in advance.

Finally, it is about time to start developing black-owned national franchise systems in new fields. The Irish became famous for their taverns, the Jews for their delicatessens, the Chinese for their laundries, the Italians for their pizza parlors and construction firms. The economic success stories of all other ethnic groups shows that they consistently built their most successful businesses by selling to their own people. There must be an economic opportunity particularly suited to blacks.

The concept of franchising could open new vistas for black people. It provides business opportunities with the ingredients for success built right in; it is ideally suited to variations like Young Entrepreneurs, Inc.; and it is infinitely expandable. If franchising is properly promoted and implemented as a part of the black business development program, it can double the number and the quality of black businesses in the next decade. **However, I cannot overemphasize the fact that one must investigate before he invests.** To assist in this evaluation, Dr. Wilford White, Director of the Small Business Guidance and Development Center at Howard University, developed a list of twenty-four questions to which everyone should secure answers before he signs any franchise agreement.

1. Did your lawyer approve the franchise contract you are considering after he studied it paragraph by paragraph?

2. Does the franchise call upon you to take any steps which are, according to your lawyer, unwise or illegal in your state, county, or city?

3. Does the franchise give you an exclusive territory for the length of the franchise or can the franchiser sell a second or third franchise in your territory?

4. Is the franchiser connected in any way with any other franchise company handling similar merchandise or services?

5. If the answer to the last question is "Yes" what is your protection against this second franchiser organization?

6. Under what circumstances can you terminate the franchise contract and at what cost to you, if you decide for any reason at all that you wish to cancel it?

7. If you sell your franchise, will you be com-

pensated for your goodwill or will the goodwill you have built into the business be lost by you?

8. For how many years has the firm offering you a franchise been in operation?

9. Has it a reputation for honesty and fair dealing among the local firms holding its franchise?

10. Has the franchiser shown you any certified figures indicating exact net profits of one or more going firms which you personally checked with the franchisee?

11. Will the firm assist you with:
    (a) A management training program?
    (b) An employee training program?
    (c) A public relations program?
    (d) Capital?
    (e) Credit?
    (f) Merchandising ideas?

12. Will the firm assist you in finding a good location for your new business?

13. Is the franchising firm adequately financed so that it can carry out its stated plan of financial assistance and expansion?

14. Is the franchiser a one-man company or a corporation with an experienced management trained in depth (so that there would always be an experienced man at its head)?

15. Exactly what can the franchiser do for you which you cannot do for yourself?

16. Has the franchiser investigated you care-

fully enough to assure itself that you can successfully operate one of their franchises at a profit both to them and to you?

17. How much equity capital will you need to purchase the franchise and operate it until your income equals your expenses? Where are you going to get it?

18. Are you prepared to give up some independence of action to secure the advantages offered by the franchise?

19. Do you really believe you have the innate ability, training, and experience to work smoothly and profitably with the franchiser, your employees, and your customers?

20. Are you ready to spend much or all of the remainder of your business life with this franchiser, offering his product or service to your public?

21. Have you made any study to determine whether the product or service which you propose to sell under franchise has a market in your territory at the prices you will have to charge?

22. Will the population in the territory given you increase, remain static, or decrease over the next five years?

23. Will the product or service you are considering be in greater demand, about the same, or less demand five years from now than today?

24. What competition in your territory already

exists for the product or service you contemplate selling? Nonfranchise firms? Franchise firms?

Although many black people apparently believe that franchising is an exploitative scheme, I am convinced that franchising offers the black community an important business opportunity. If the franchising system is properly applied, it can produce thousands of black entrepreneurs in a relatively short time. But, as attractive as franchising may be under some circumstances, it is not a panacea. No single approach is a cure-all for the troubles of the black business community. Many approaches must be developed if we are to expect progress.

6   THE TRANSFER

It used to be axiomatic that everyone who lived in the ghetto was black and everyone who owned a business in the ghetto was white. Even in Harlem, it wasn't until 1964 that a black man actually owned a business in a prime section of 125th Street. In community after community the turf had been divided up before the black man got there. As the neighborhood changed from white to black, white businessmen moved their families to other neighborhoods, but they kept their grocery stores and clothing shops in the ghetto. And even though in many cases the black man felt he was receiving inferior merchandise and paying higher prices, he patronized these stores and so the white-owned business survived.

But the urban upheavals of the 1960s drastically

changed the face of business in the black community. Many white businessmen decided that the cost and risk of doing business had become too high and so they left in hordes. Today 14th Street in Washington, D.C., is lined with store fronts that have been boarded up or burned out or barred in, and similar shells line the streets of Watts and Hough and Roxbury. Many other white businessmen are hanging on only because they don't want to abandon what amounts to a life's work and they would move out tomorrow if they could find a buyer.

The chance to buy an existing business, therefore, could be an attractive prospect for many black businessmen. Many black people say, "Don't buy white folks' trash," but to me the "trash" that a white businessman took forty years to build can be very profitable to a black businessman who would otherwise have to spend forty years himself. Again, it is simply bad business to do work that has already been done.

Putting a new business together is a very involved and difficult job, but the task is probably twice as hard in the center city—and twice again as hard in the ghetto. Sizable parcels of land are difficult to assemble, building is expensive, credit and insurance are almost impossible to get, so buying an existing business has many advantages:

The land, buildings, equipment, and inventory are already there. Some face-lifting and redecoration might be in order, but that is a minor task in comparison with starting from scratch.

The vital relationships between the business and its suppliers, its bank, its insurance company, and so forth, are already established and intact.

Employees are already hired, trained, and proven; thus, the new owner not only avoids the expensive and time-consuming process of hiring and training, but he is less likely to be saddled with the high turnover which typically occurs among new employees.

A market has already been established. Presumably the first owner found the market in the area to be fertile; the new owner can keep the readymade clientele and probably enlarge it.

Finally, and most important, the new owner has the advice and counsel of his predecessor. This built-in management assistance includes expertise in the traditional areas of accounting, taxation, marketing, and so forth, but it also includes the great body of informal, first-hand know-how that the businessman has accumulated over years of experience. This second kind of assistance is unique to the buyout situation. It could not be obtained from any other source.

Despite all these advantages which would be included in the ideal buyout case, the black man who is thinking of purchasing an existing business has to look out for some hazards and disadvantages:

First and most important is the assumption that the business will run at least as profitably under new (black) ownership. I remember one deal that appeared to be extremely promising: the old owner was buying beverages at 15 percent less than the average wholesale price and retailing them competitively—thus turning a net profit 15 percent above average. It was only after the papers were signed and the new owner tried to buy inventory that he found the old owner belonged to a mass buying clique that had a standing 10-for-the-price-of-8 deal—and blacks were not welcome in the clique. That's only one kind of surprise that can result from failure to investigate a buyout business thoroughly before investing.

Another surprise involves the price of an existing firm. Ghetto buyout deals are so submerged in fear and ignorance that the price is seldom a "fair" one: either the new owner is getting a real bargain as the white man flees the ghetto, or the old owner is gouging the black man under the guise of a bargain sacrifice.

When an exchange of ownership occurs under such hostile conditions, it is no surprise that a previous owner isn't eager to pass on his expertise and experience to the black entrepreneur. Not only does this mean that one of the key advantages of buyouts is lost, but it can mean that the new owner is immediately crippled; he hasn't been introduced to the firm's banker, insurance agent, suppliers, and so forth, and in general he may not know where to start.

In my opinion, these problems could be eliminated and the full potential of buyouts could be realized more often if a local black business development agency could act as transfer agent for the deals.

The agent would develop a file of businessmen willing to sell for a fair market price; similarly, the agent would try to match opportunities with appropriate prospective black entrepreneurs. This sounds deceptively easy; the organization I am describing would have to be very familiar with the local business community and the black community. They would have to be trusted by each, and would have to possess a considerable amount of business and advisory skill.

After bringing the two parties together, the agent would have the responsibility of arbitrating to set a fair market price on the business. This doesn't even sound easy; real estate and equipment prices, especially in the ghetto and under the pressures described above, are extremely capricious.

Nevertheless, I feel there is one method that could solve these problems and definitely should be used: a selling price based on future earnings and paid in installments only as the "new business" establishes that it is profitable. This is the only approach that is consistent with general business principles, it is completely apolitical and eliminates fear and threats from the deal. This method has the further advantage of providing an incentive to the old owner to help make the new business as profitable as possible as soon as possible, while placing full final control in the hands of the new owner.

The transfer agent should remain on the scene after the deal is made. Having been integrally involved in the investigation and negotiation phases, he would be well suited for sponsoring follow-up management assistance and monitoring. The agent would not necessarily have to use its own staff of consultants, but could work with other business development groups and community organizations, adult training centers, and universities, bringing in whatever help the new entrepreneur would need.

In most cities such a transfer agent does not exist; further, the necessity that such an institution be impartial, universally trusted, and politically independent eliminates most of the groups in any given city that might be candidates for filling the role.

One present possibility exists: local black banks. They are close to the community and are already involved in financial dealings with minority businessmen; they should, therefore, be familiar with both existing and potential businessmen in the community. Perhaps most important, they have a natural interest in promoting new, viable black ownership in the community. That interest would not only motivate them to actively promote fair buyout deals, but in the case of an eventual bankruptcy, a black bank would be more likely to preserve the business under a new owner rather than liquidate it.

There are other candidates for the transfer agent function: SBA's Minority Enterprise Small Business Investment Company and Local Development Company programs offer formalized structures that might be suitable; or, on the other hand, very ambitious and talented individual promoters might be able to fill the role.

Specifics will necessarily vary from city to city, but the general concept must be implemented as a part of any local black business development effort.

And, of course, the transfer agency itself should act as a creative instrument for the orderly transfer of businesses from white to black ownership. Here is one opportunity that the transfer agent might encourage. Traditionally, fathers pass their businesses on to their sons. Although few black youngsters have fathers or mothers who own businesses, many black youngsters work for white owners who either have no children or whose children have no interest in the business. The transfer agent could supervise a procedure through which the black youngster inherits the business.

Let's say, for example, that a black pharmacist agrees to work for an established, white-owned drug-store soon after he finishes college. He and the white owner enter into an agreement in which X dollars will be deducted from his pay every week and placed into a special bank account supervised by the transfer agent. The white owner contributes an additional X dollars a week to the fund himself. The black pharmacist is taking home a little less but he is buying an option to own his own business. The present owner is paying out a little more but he has an assistant who has a long-term interest in the successful operation of the business. At any time the black can withdraw from the plan and remove his share of the money from the account. He can also withdraw a share of the owner's matching money as well, according to a formula based on how long he has held the job. But if he decides to leave the money in the account, the black pharmacist is accumulating a fund—his contribution and the owner's—which after a certain number of years he will use as equity capital to buy the business.

Black communities have suffered under outside ownership of "their" businesses, but they will suffer even more if those businesses are abandoned without replacement. The transfer agent proposed can prevent the death of existing companies and turn them into the base for a rebirth of business—black-owned business—in the black community.

NATIONAL TRANSFERS

The black community cannot forever feed on itself, however. Although the ghetto-business pie was cut long ago, even then it was not a pie of manufacturing, distribution, and business service firms. If black business is ever to become more significant than a collection of carryouts and dry-cleaning firms, black men will have to enter the industries that are the backbone of mainstream commerce: manufacturing, wholesale supply, durables retailing—all the fields in which blacks are now conspicuously absent.

When we talk in terms of a national program, thus implying large numbers of ownership transfers, we must concentrate on the smaller firms in the less sophisticated fields because there just isn't a large number of highly qualified and educated blacks who are capable of assuming ownership of huge corporations.

But because new businesses are so very difficult to create, and because new black businesses could probably never grow fast enough to "catch up," the part of our program that will improve the quality of black business must concentrate on buying existing large businesses—such is the only path to real diversification and strength.

Thus there clearly must be two approaches to black business development: many relatively small firms in relatively traditional business areas, and fewer large corporations in the forefront of relatively new and major industries.

While there has been progress in the first area, small businesses, relatively little effort has been devoted to large business. I feel this has been a failure of two groups: the challenge stands clearly addressed to the growing ranks of young blacks blessed with entrepreneurial talent and, again, to corporate business leaders in America.

If there is to be any quantum improvement in the quality and significance of black business in the next decade, young blacks in graduate schools and junior executive ranks will have to formulate management teams and dedicate themselves to spearheading the climb to power; mainstream businessmen will have to recognize the need to integrate business ownership at the national and international levels as well as at the street-corner level.

I personally think black ownership of major corporations is in a stage analogous to the pre-four-minute mile. The barriers are imaginary, blacks do not control any significant corporations simply because blacks have never controlled any significant corporation. There are no real barriers but dedication; once a single black team has dedicated itself to becoming the spearhead, once the relatively small but eminently talented cadre of young black businessmen repudiate the hollow privilege of selling their brains to others and successfully take over the management responsibility of a major corporation, the imaginary barrier will be broken, precedent will be set, and blacks from that time hence will have a major achievement to which they can aspire: a piece of the real action.

There is a need for a helping mechanism here, too; it should be a transfer agent just like the one described earlier but working on a national scale and dealing exclusively with larger businesses. A wealth of experience has been developed. Dedicated white companies have attempted turn-key and sponsorship arrangements for transferring control to blacks, but with only limited success so far. The recent merger and acquisition trend has spun off a wealth of expertise on the problems and proprieties of installing new management.

Now all this immensely technical and complicated experience should be collected and studied, then hammered into a comprehensive package of ownership transfer techniques. Then the national transfer agent should apply its transfer package on behalf of mutually interested mainstream-and-minority negotiators to facilitate the transfer of at least two or three large businesses per year. The methods need not be Draconian. Installing black faces in all the top slots just for the sake of demonstration would probably result in a turbulent complex of emotional problems and disturbance. The changeover should be 100 percent business profit oriented. There are blacks who are qualified and willing to become masters rather than slaves of big business, but only now have they been able to enter the mainstream of capitalism—about one hundred years too late.

The transfer mechanisms I have described would attempt to bridge those one hundred years with expertise and courage; they would represent a crucial part of the effort to make meaningful ownership opportunity a reality for black men.

7   THE UNIVERSITY

In my view of the world the university has always held a very special position, and I think that it should take a top spot on any list of potential contributors to the cause of black business development. The university is made up of young, active, concerned students who require only guidance and a channel for their abundant energies; its teachers represent some of the most innovative thinking in America; its research and educational facilities may well hold the answers to our most urgent questions; its administration has the confidence of business and government leaders; and the university provides an atmosphere of reason and objectivity which inspires respect throughout the world.

Yes, universities have contributed vital ideas for improvement of our society, but they have limited their efforts to a very narrow area. Their research for the government has concentrated on science, foreign affairs, weapon development, but seldom anything as mundane as small business, particularly small black business.

In short, too many universities have remained aloof from the many crucial issues and needs around them —and students have had to force this recognition. Where I have found courses on black economic development, on the grass-roots political climate, on innovative answers to urban problems, they have been student-conceived, student-led courses. The young men and women who return from summers in Headstart, in the government, in the ghettos, bring with them a true concern and a realistic picture of what is happening in this country. By translating their concern into campus action they are slowly bringing down the ivory towers—and they should be congratulated for it.

UNIVERSITIES AND BLACK BUSINESS DEVELOPMENT

Throughout this book I have emphasized that a lack of knowledge of business systems and procedures is one of the major problems facing black business development. Obviously, the one institution in our society that is best equipped to correct that lack of knowledge is the university. But how relevant are universities to black business development today?

Their primary responsibility is education—preparing young people for socially and personally rewarding roles in society—yet only one major black university is an accredited member of the American Association of Collegiate Schools of Business. Only 119 blacks graduated from the seventeen leading graduate schools of business in 1969—and that number is seventeen times the number of blacks graduated in 1963.[1]

Isn't business a socially rewarding role? In my opinion, a cadre of well-trained, bright and ambitious young blacks could transform the economic life of any ghetto in America. Isn't business a personally rewarding career? Corporations have bid so aggressively for black business managers that statistics show the average black manager can earn more per year of school than the average black doctor.

Why, then, do universities, especially black universities, perpetuate an educational program that virtually ignores business for black students? How can they become more relevant?

Independent research is perhaps the second most important activity of the university. The few studies of black businesses that exist repeatedly begin at the ground floor and work up to a level that is still relatively broad, general, and, in many cases, irrelevant. If a serious research effort were undertaken in this area, soon we could concentrate on the more sophisticated questions in black business development that are crying for answers. What are the political implications for autonomous community development agencies versus

[1] "MBA Magazine," April–May 1969 (New York: MBA Enterprises. Inc., 1969), p. 11.

those controlled by the mayor's office? Indeed, what is the relationship between black employment/median income in the ghetto and black-owned ghetto business? These and thousands of other questions are in desperate need of sophisticated research. Students, faculty members, and the whole black business effort could profit from serious attention to such issues.

The third activity of the university is formal consulting and advising. Fortunately, in this area many individuals and groups associated with the university have been active; a few have even contributed to the field of minority business. Unfortunately, not enough students have been involved so far. They should be.

Through black business consulting, business students in particular have a valuable opportunity to contribute to the community and enhance their learning experience. Harvard, MIT, Columbia, Stanford, and a few other business schools have developed consulting teams in recent years; the teams involve students supported by faculty members who volunteer their time to counsel and advise minority businessmen. They assist in loan applications, discuss long-range goals, teach rudimentary accounting skills, suggest display and promotional programs, and so forth. The students don't always have the expertise and understanding that comes from business experience, but they bring a fresh, analytical approach to small local businesses; the knowledge of basic business skills that they do possess is often welcome information to the small businessman. Thus, the business consulting program becomes a worthwhile academic learning experience for both parties as well as a lesson in human communication.

A PLAN FOR UNIVERSITY INVOLVEMENT

Unfortunately, the current attitude in the university does not encourage full commitment to such programs. Too often, consulting must be extracurricular. And the problem, of course, is that when academic credit is not given, students cannot use their full time and resources to support the program. In most cases, consulting programs with academic credit are limited to one or two semesters, becoming completely inactive during the summer months; thus continuity is lost and the black businessmen begin to question the sincerity of the program. Finally, most plans are crippled by a total lack of financial as well as academic incentives.

If the university is to become truly and effectively involved in the black economic development effort, students and black businessmen will have to initiate plans and appeals to institutionalize active involvement. If they propose a sound plan for involvement, they will undoubtedly find interest and support not only from the university but also from the government and foundations and possibly from big business. There are several pilot projects that can provide experience and guidance for such a plan; Ford Foundation and Harvard University have collaborated on student consulting programs. Columbia University has been active in consulting for several years; MIT has offered assistance to minority businessmen through a combination of classroom instruction and individual consulting advice.

Howard University has gone further than any, however. And since its experience has come closest to a total approach, I would offer Howard's programs as a beginning model. The Small Business Guidance and Development Center grew out of a proposal developed jointly by representatives of the U.S. Commerce Department and Howard University in the spring of 1964. They agreed that the Center should be organized and operated to help improve the management skills of the growing number of small businessmen in metropolitan Washington, D.C. The objective was to increase sales and receipts, employment and profits and thus give the businessmen more time for greater community service participation. The Center was intended to serve business people of all races although the founders assumed that it would primarily serve blacks. Subsequent checks indicate that about 85 percent of the clients are black.

The first director of the Center was chosen for his experience with small business. He was Dr. Wilford White, who had previously been Assistant Deputy Administrator for SBA in charge of management assistance. Three professional counselors, a secretary, a clerk-typist, and a full-time librarian completed the staff. The staff was backed up by an advisory committee of twelve, elected from the faculty of Howard and the Washington business community. The committee monitored progress of the Center and recommended changes in policy, programs, and procedure.

The Center initially offered two basic programs: Individual Counseling/Group Counseling and Management Assistance. The immediate demand for such services was impressive: By the close of the first quarter, the Center had provided counseling on request from owners of such businesses as a trucking service, used-car lot, restaurant, sales promotion firm, dry-cleaning plant, exterminating business, home improvement business, household appliance store, shoe repair shop, tire-retreading shop, music school, sign manufacturer, specialty bakery, glass ornaments retailer, welder, beauty parlor, and a furniture refinisher.

The Center ingeniously harnessed the demand for advice by bringing owners of similar businesses together in problem clinics. It started with a problem clinic for black members of the construction industry.

The first problem which the contractors brought to the Center was, "Now that it is fall, how do we find new customers so that we can keep our trained men working during the winter months?" A conference meeting was held and out of it emerged thirteen acceptable ideas. These ideas were reproduced and distributed before the close of the session. The results were so highly valued by the businessmen that other sessions were held approximately twice a month to discuss other subjects such as, "Where can I find new employees?'' "What sources of funds are available to contractors?'' and "How can we improve our images as businessmen?''

All of the problem clinics have used these procedures: groups—not more than fifteen; conference format—no speakers; subjects are selected by the businessmen one meeting ahead; informal special guests are invited at the request of members—to answer questions only; meetings held at various locations; open agenda—members can bring up related subjects at all times; "highlights" are distributed to all members prior to the close of each meeting and mailed to those not present.

The clinics in all fields have proven quite successful. From the Center's standpoint, they are a perfect vehicle for dispensing advice efficiently because they gather several clients at once; for the clients, the clinics are valuable because they supply a mixture of formal academic information and informal practical experience.

Most important, perhaps, the clinics are a perfect beginning for business organizations described in Chapter 4. By working toward such self-perpetuating grass roots institutions, the Center has transcended typical business advisory services and established something infinitely more valuable.

At the close of the first year, the Center was counseling seventy-five prospective and actual business owners and conducting training programs that reached over three hundred owners of smaller business firms in metropolitan Washington. Once programs were established to care for the basic and immediate needs of the small businessmen, the Center was able to expand its curriculum to more sophisticated topics. For instance, an eight-week administrative management course was developed and taught in cooperation with the SBA. Ideally, such courses would include lessons offered by local banks, investment houses, real estate brokers, and other relevant business service institutions as well as the mainstream business firms in the community. Eventually a comprehensive formal adult education curriculum should be offered. But the important step was beginning at the level of immediate needs and interests and gradually upgrading to the normal level of university education.

It became apparent very early in the Howard experience that manuals outlining the successful programs would be valuable for future efforts as well as for other schools and institutions interested in replicating the Center. Fortunately, such manuals have been prepared and are available to interested parties (a list is offered in the Appendix).

This successful Howard University experience provides a number of useful lessons for other interested organizations. First is the point already made: business assistance must start at the educational level of the client-pupil; with small businessmen, especially blacks, that level is not usually as high as the normal university standard.

Second, the Center found that accepting all comers

was not a fruitful policy; some effort should be made to screen applicants, primarily to determine their real motivation. Howard's experience showed that motivation and goals varied so much between older and younger businessmen that applicants had to be divided into two parallel groups, split along an age line of about forty-five years. Because younger clients were much more flexible and thus benefited more from advice, all assistance programs tried to concentrate on the younger group.

Third, all assistance should be offered on a business basis with a fee for services rendered, not as charity. A fee not only insures the sincerity of the client, but establishes a healthier relationship between the client and the adviser.

Fourth, meaningful progress for a black entrepreneur frequently requires more than revision of his procedures. The greatest need of almost all black businessmen is breaking into the general mainstream market. All consulting advice should be oriented toward accomplishing that. It is the opinion of the Center that blacks can operate successfully in the general market in almost any manufacturing, wholesale, retail, or service trade—**if** proper attention is paid to price, quality, and service. The Center encourages prospective black businessmen to enter those areas of business where black business is particularly uncommon but where a strong market exists. In so doing, the Center creates more problems by generating the need for much more management assistance, but in the long run it forces more significant changes in the pattern and quality of black business.

Fifth, the biggest problem clients bring to the Center is lack of motivation. Many of them backed into business or were driven into it by a desire to avoid retirement, to "show up the boss," to make a fast fortune, or to "get a job" in the face of employment discrimination. Thus, many black businessmen are not entrepreneurs at all. Realizing their inadequacies, they do not aspire to very high achievement, but rather accept low earnings and rationalize them by aggressively asserting their independence, albeit empty. For instance, the Center has not yet found a way to convince many clients of the value of financial records. Clients still feel that records are confusing, time-consuming, expensive, and quite unnecessary since an owner should always have the business "in his head." Clients limit their outlook to the four walls of their stores. They still don't take much positive interest in community problems, even when those problems affect their businesses.

So far, the best solution to the motivation problem has been retreat sessions. About fourteen clients are sent to a learning center located in a quiet rural environment. There, the businessmen are stimulated according to a rigorous, tested program to think about opportunities for starting or expanding their businesses. They are encouraged to come out of the experience with definite goals and a fresh, clear idea of how to proceed immediately with implementation.

Perhaps the biggest mistake that the Howard Center made at the start was its failure to involve enthusiastic students in the project. The Center has since corrected that mistake and has also come to realize that minority business assistance requires not only business students, but also students from law school and students from the graduate and undergraduate departments of economics, sociology, architecture, accounting, and politics. Student interest in the issues and problems of the day cuts across department lines and extends far beyond routine course work.

Sincere student enthusiasm, in fact, could prove to be the greatest untapped resource of all in our universities. All through the 1960s students challenged the ability of the American system to cope with America's problems. Some students were so alienated that they felt that they had to attack the system, and indeed the university, violently. But a far larger group wants to find ways in which the capitalist system itself can solve the problems. What better way could we find than by allowing those youngsters to put their talents into aiding black economic development? The benefits to the black community will be long-range as well as short-range. The more whites we can reach and make aware of the problems of the black businessman before they are desensitized by the spirit-numbing routines of the white bureaucracy, the more friends the black business community will have in the future and the better off it will be.

Black business development is an ideal way for universities to get themselves and their students involved. Universities exist to serve society. There is no need more important today than the repair of our social fabric, which has been ripped by racial and ethnic inequality. Universities exist to serve their communities. There is no better way for universities to step out of their ivory towers and cooperate as neighbors than by assisting community members in need. Universities exist to serve their students. Students want to become involved in social action, deserve to be shown how their formal knowledge can apply to the real world, and will enhance their knowledge by learning from example. Finally, universities exist to serve themselves. They rightly try to enlarge their own prestige and educating capability in every move they make. I firmly believe that minority business assistance is consistent with all these university goals. I further think that university involvement in black business and other social problem areas deserves to be institutionalized.

The experiences of Howard University's Center are just suggestions for a beginning. Similar and expanded involvement could take place in many areas of current social action through the establishment of what I might call the university's Social Action Task Force. Such a program would bring together the nation's needs and the universities' goals and unique facilities by:

(a) defining specific areas of social need and declaring volunteer work in these areas as a legitimate academic interest for members of the university community.

(b) allowing part time consulting or "junior year in the community" internship work to be counted as fully or partially equal to academic or teaching credit, provided it were conducted as part of a formalized program of academic and social worth.

(c) encouraging work-study projects to be incorporated into relevant courses and supporting summer jobs in community service areas.

The university Social Action Task Force program could be given continuity and could benefit from continuing feedback by incorporating a fellowship program. Students or faculty members would be employed as interns in government or private social action organizations for perhaps eighteen months, then would return to the university for six months to collect and publish their experiences and would remain in the university for a final year as coordinators and administrators of the university Social Action program.

The idea of isolating some of our freshest and most energetic citizens in an ivy-walled institution when they would rather be relating their knowledge to the world's problems and making their contribution to society is, in my mind, a tremendous waste of resources. Although I am not qualified as an educator, I can see little sense in the traditional idea of packing detached knowledge into captive bodies for four years, then disgorging those bodies into the "real" world, never to return. If the futurists among us are right and the next decades will see the university move closer and closer to the center of daily American life, the time to begin serious university involvement is now. If today's students are truly the vanguard of a new America, if they seriously envision a society substantially better than the one they see beyond the ivy walls, then the time to take their energies beyond those walls is now. If alienation is a common denominator that moves men to action, students and blacks will continue to move, to awaken to the social action that this country so desperately needs. I sincerely hope that the ideas of this chapter will help them to move together.

8   PROMOTION AND DELIVERY

The community organization plays a crucial role in the development of black business, for in many cases, without the community organization the man and the resources would simply never meet one another.

The Prudential Life Insurance Company, for example, says that it is willing to invest up to $1 million in its Minority Small Business Investment Company that makes loans to black businessmen in need of help. But by itself that offer, generous though it may be, has little meaning to Joe Smith, the black tradesman on Market Street in lower Newark. To him Prudential is an imposing mass of stone that might as well be a castle in Spain as a corporate headquarters in downtown Newark. Smith is afraid to go inside and ask for help. He doesn't know what to wear and he feels that he wouldn't know what to say. Quite simply, he is terrified that he would make a fool of himself. On the other side, the executives of Prudential don't know that Joe Smith exists and if they did, they might find it difficult to understand his problems.

Therefore, we need the community development organization that can speak to both Prudential and to Joe Smith. Without the community development organization the connection would never be made, the circuit would never be closed, the energy would never be transmitted.

Still, the community organizations are not doing all that they might do. It's not for lack of goodwill. There are certainly thousands of individuals, businesses, churches, foundations, schools, and governments that have something to offer. But they have not yet been organized in an effective way. What is lacking in black business development today is a unified, coordinated, efficient delivery mechanism that can pull together all the resources that are available, package them into worthwhile and effective programs, and take them to the local scene where they are so desperately needed. Again, what we need is a promoter, or a host of promoters who can take the props and the players, the stage and the script, and get the show on the road.

The role of promoter naturally falls to the national black leadership groups. Black leaders and their organizations have already started filling the role and the programs and the organizations that they have formed show great promise. Unfortunately, however, much of that promise is being lost because of common operational problems and a lack of communication among the thousands of people involved in business development across the country.

In this chapter, I want to look at business development organizations in a spirit of constructive analysis because I feel that increased cooperation, clear mutual understanding, and a few major adjustments can bring black and white organizations closer to realizing their full potential in the vital promoter role.

OPERATIONAL PROBLEMS

The first major operational problem, as I see it, is usually found in those organizations that are relatively old, have established a track record in civil rights, and are now attempting to operate with a diversity of objectives. They have come to feel that they must "do something" in business development to remain relevant, strong, and popular. So after years of using civil rights tactics in the civil rights field, they either eliminate some of their old programs or, more commonly, try to expand their scope into the business development field.

The result is twofold: First, in their expansion to a new field, they too frequently try to keep their old civil rights tactics. Unfortunately, businesses are not created by teaching sit-in, voter registration, or court-case techniques to the masses; they are created by teaching business systems and procedures to individuals. These civil rights organizations too often just don't have business expertise and understanding. Further, such organizations inevitably dilute their efforts in their original field of operation, such as voter registration, thus wasting the expertise and understanding that they do have.

The second major operational problem occurs in business development organizations that try to function on several levels at once. Some attempt to become the entire resource pipeline: they solicit, digest, repackage, distribute, and install resources all by themselves. While this would appear to be a logical and efficient approach, the organizations that have tried it have lost effectiveness at both ends. By trying to relate to mainstream and minority communities at the same time, they have lost credibility, understanding, and effectiveness in both communities—they cannot stay close enough to the white corporate and financial communities to obtain a maximum commitment of resources. They cannot retain the close confidence and perspective of the black community that is necessary to function as a grass-roots citizen. Further, by stretching their personnel and their administrative funds beyond practical limits, they weaken the general efforts of the organization.

A third major problem is common to the organizations that operate on a national scope and try to centralize their organizational control and operational leadership. These are the "top down" organizations with strong central policy-making bodies that expect local branches to do nothing more than carry out centrally established tasks toward centrally established objectives. Not only do such organizations obviously show a lack of confidence in local leadership, but they implicitly confess a lack of contact with local branches. As a natural consequence, local issues and specialized needs are ignored and programs are designed and perpetuated without the benefit of feedback and evaluation from the local scene. Thus, such a structure completely eliminates any chance of developing strong local leadership cadres; the program just is not flexible enough to retain the allegiance of talented men.

The greatest danger of the centralized national organization is that its leaders will feel obliged to write **the** definitive strategy for black business development; such a strategy inevitably ends up describing how one organization, the author's, will handle all the needs and problems that face black business development. But no one organization has or can have all the resources and all the answers. What is needed instead is a coordinated, multifaceted, joint effort that allows all national organizations to pool their strengths and make them available for bottom-up, locally tailored programs.

The final problem is on the local level. It involves the dimensions of political orientation, operational leadership, and organizational control that have been mentioned above in a national context. Briefly, the local problem is one of representation: in order to relate to a broad range of institutions and individuals (both resource and recipient), the local organization will either attempt to include both whites and blacks in equal numbers, or will gather as diverse a range of black leadership as possible on the board of directors. In either case, there are problems.

If control is shared by blacks and whites, the organization is immediately perceived as establishment-initiated and white-dominated. The less militant blacks join, but those who might be termed "constructively militant" refuse to associate themselves with the organization for fear of losing their strength and credibility. As a consequence, power and control in the organization slides to establishment members and the organization finds itself unable to relate its programs to the needs of the man-on-the-street, yet unaware of its failings because of lack of contact with the community.

If control is invested in an all-black board, but the board attempts to amalgamate too broad a sample of black leadership, the organization may become operationally paralyzed. The potential of many strong leaders is wasted as each maneuvers to satisfy his personal interests and the desires of his particular constituents. A narrow sample of black leadership can avoid this paralysis, but usually suffers from a lack of talent, experience, and credibility in the broader community.

There is obviously a very delicate balance to be sought by the local organization. My own feeling is that only when one individual has the charisma and ability to command a local "machine" can a single local organization perform efficiently. Lacking such an individual, the local scene, like the national one, must be a pluralistic amalgam of many voluntarily coordinated, specialized, groups.

The solutions that I would recommend for these operational problems are implicit in the above descriptions, but to summarize:

I envision the effective promoter/delivery mechanism as a structure in which all business development groups, black and white, work together according to four mutually accepted principles:

Strict business development orientation. All groups resolve to operate strictly toward the goal of viability and profitability for existing and new black businesses; non-business goals and tactics that belong more properly to social welfare, area economic development, or civil rights efforts are relegated to secondary priority.

Division of labor. All groups recognize the three distinct steps in the resource pipeline—supplier who furnishes or solicits resources for the wholesaler, wholesaler who coordinates and packages resources into a form appropriate for the retailer, and retailer who channels these resources to the individual entrepreneur—they limit their roles to one level or the segment of one level that they are most capable of executing.

White involvement at the resource level. White individuals and institutions attempt to limit their participation to marshaling and providing resources, thus avoiding direct involvement in the local retail organizations, except for technical assistance when needed.

Bottom-up emphasis. All groups recognize the need

for programs and power to emanate from the grass roots local level.

UNMET NEEDS

A promoter/delivery mechanism designed and functioning along the lines outlined above would go a long way toward molding the black business development effort into a coherent, effective attack. Yet even with such cooperation, there will be unmet needs and unsolved problems.

Obviously the key to the delivery mechanism outlined above is coordination. Although a single coordinating office would be neither desirable nor effective if it sprang from one of the existing black business development groups, some forum for agreement on principles and division of labor will be necessary.

Information is presently scarce. The minority community is relatively unaware of the untapped resources available in its own midst and of the business opportunities and resources available through cooperation with mainstream sources of assistance. The mainstream community lacks knowledge of proper ways to "get involved" in black business development and, in some cases, still lacks the information that will illustrate the social and self-interested gains that can be made through a commitment to black business development. Even after the creation of an effective delivery mechanism, a clearinghouse and propagator for such information will be necessary.

A lack of knowledge of business systems and procedures is certainly the major problem at the grass roots level, but it is a deficiency throughout the resource pipeline as well. A training facility for business development leaders and a "sensitivity" center for mainstream activists are probably needed just as much as a facility for motivation and education of individual entrepreneurs.

Finally, the special conditions of the black community, especially the ghetto, require that a number of special although temporary new devices be formed as generators and channelers of resources that presently are not available through other institutions. I am thinking specifically of the desperate need for equity capital, casualty and surety insurance, mass purchasing power, franchise information, buyout expertise, and so forth.

The realization that these and probably other needs are not being filled by present programs argues strongly for some type of new machinery or institution to round out the black business development structure.

9   NEW MODELS

Performing musicians employ other musicians, behind-the-scenes players who never appear before an audience and who never cut a record. Still, these unseen, unheard "musician's musicians" play a vital role in the making of music. They write the scores and run the rehearsals and without them there would simply be no performance, no music.

Black business needs a "musician's musician" who will guide its performance. Black business needs a "company's company," which will serve the company, promote the economic advancement of black people, accelerate entry into the general business community, study black economic needs, develop and test new innovative approaches, disseminate its research, stimulate the development of an entrepreneurial class, and become a self-perpetuating organization independent of the erratic off-again, on-again support of federal agencies and private companies and foundations.

The agencies that most need help are the business development organizations. It is at this level in black business development that the would-be black entrepreneur is able to identify possible resources and shape his ideas into a viable business concept. Thus, the primary role of this "musician's musician" would be to score the procedures for the business development organizations. It is certain that without this kind of guidance the business development organizations will drift without proper coordination and direction and the entire black business movement will founder.

I would call this new servant the Institute for Economic Action. The Institute might be headquartered at an existing institution such as Howard University which already has under one roof all of the disciplines necessary for the creation and implementation of economic development plans: bankers, lawyers, accountants, and business administrators. The Institute would have to be a separate unit within the business school of whatever university was chosen and it would have its own permanent chair. Further, it would be organized as a nonprofit corporation under the laws of, say, the District of Columbia and have a board of about fifteen people, four from industry, nine from business development organizations, and two from the academic community. Public and private funds of about $15 million would be required to get the Institute started and after that the Institute would have to develop its own capability to tap resources, including of course those of the businesses it serves. But at the beginning the Small Business Administration, the Office of Economic Opportunity, the Department of Labor, the Office of Minority Business Enterprise, and the Office of Education should all be approached for funds.

Some of its functions would be to serve as:

A forum. To bring black business development organizations together so that they can establish a consensus on definitions of goals and objectives, division of effort and specialization, and long-range strategy. Thus, to coordinate while remaining subordinate to each major business development organization.

A clearinghouse. To provide a clearinghouse and a propagator of vital information: (a) program ideas—examples of projects proposed and/or implemented at the local or national level, ideally with analysis and evaluation of such ideas; (b) bootstrap opportunities —specific businesses or markets that offer opportunity for black ownership; (c) available resources—both resources that are now available in mainstream and minority communities, and resources that could be generated through meaningful appeal and planning; and (d) new ideas—the results by both the new servant organization and outside groups. Thus, to provide active communications channels among grass-roots groups and individuals, national organizations, and interested mainstream bodies.

A planner. To plan, instigate, and furnish or sponsor educational programs and facilities:
  (a) for general entrepreneurial motivation and skills,
  (b) for specific technical skills,
  (c) for business development techniques, and
  (d) for "sensitivity" orientation.

To develop sources of assistance, new program ideas, and new devices for channeling resources.

We need, in short, a combination think-tank and community stimulator, functioning primarily as a servant organization to respond to needs expressed by business development organizations. For example, let's review a few of the types of projects the Institute for Economic Action might structure, implement, and direct for business development organizations:

A credit pool and guaranty project. To help solve the problem of getting commercial bank business loans, the new servant organization might consider a loan guaranty pool similar to one that was established by a local New York organization, the Association to Assist Negro Business. Their pool is capitalized by pledges from local businesses, churches, and other institutions and is available for collateral purposes to minority businessmen who cannot get loans from traditional capital sources without a 100 percent loan guaranty.

Responsibility for defaulted loans is shared by all the contributors to the pool, thus the loss to any single person is relatively small; eventually, the small fees charged for guaranties will accumulate, replace the pledges, and make the pool self-perpetuating. It's a beautiful idea and it fills a crucial need; the credit pool is exactly the sort of program that should be developed by the servant organization and installed in every major city through black leadership organization.

PROJECT BOSS (Business Opportunities Search and Selection)

Back in 1964–65, the National Urban League developed a program which they called a National Skills Bank. This operation was designed to solicit resumes from many individuals around the country who were looking for suitable employment opportunities. As a result of this project, the Urban League was able to help a large number of black people who had been unable to find the right jobs, while at the same time it was able to move many others into better jobs.

We have a similar problem today in the business opportunities program. Finding the man is a most difficult task. There should be developed within the private sector a national effort designed to identify potential entrepreneurs. In thinking about this proposal, I met with Berkeley Burrell, president of the National Business League, and discussed the need and the possibility of such a project. It was his idea that we call this operation Project BOSS.

In essence, this project is designed to locate persons interested in going into business. It would get from the prospect a simple resume, a financial statement, and a statement of business objectives. It would in turn inform the prospect of business opportunities, rewards, and responsibilities. This operation would function through the local offices of participating business development organizations. Applications from prospects would be forwarded from the local communities to the Institute which would act as the national repository.

THE NATIONAL FRANCHISE DEVELOPMENT COUNCIL

In developing its franchising program, the U.S. Department of Commerce concentrated on getting major franchisers to open up specific opportunities for minorities. While this effort has been relatively successful, franchising still has not been taken out of the talking stage and delivered to minority peoples as a solid opportunity to go into business. I think part of the problem lies in the fact that the franchisers are looking to the government as a source for delivering the man, the money, and the technical assistance. They see government as the operational program head for each of the above areas. One approach that might correct this is to have the franchise industry itself, along with the minority community, establish the necessary machinery not only to make franchising a realistic opportunity but to pull together the needed resources to complete the opportunity. I would suggest that we establish a National Franchise Development Council. Again, the Institute would organize this Council solely to meet the needs of community organizations. It would have an operating staff which would carry out the following functions: (a) They would help the community organizations develop franchising opportunities, (b) convene meetings between interested minority persons and the franchisers, (c) review and give final approval on deals between minorities and franchisers, (d) solicit and screen franchise opportunities, (e) clear, review, and set standards for participating franchisers in the Council's program, (f) develop a franchise data book comprising a listing of all of those franchisers making available opportunities to minorities, including data such as amount of money needed and training provided, (g) maintain franchiser packets regarding participating franchisers which include simple instructions, brochures, and a listing of minority franchises, (h) maintain and make available a library and reference service, (i) conduct and convene seminars on franchising to be delivered in local communities through OMBE affiliates, and (j) assist minorities who have successful businesses develop and become franchiser enterprises. While this approach is similar to the Franchise Opportunity Center discussed in Chapter 5, it is recommended as an alternative approach to be designed and implemented by the Council.

In conclusion, the National Franchise Development Council would become that institution in the private sector established primarily to promote and develop franchising as a realistic opportunity for minorities to enter business.

THE MINORITY ENTERPRISE
DEVELOPMENT CORPORATION

Many minority group members in the local communities have been highly critical of franchising. They say that franchising is an illusory opportunity. They say that the initial investments are exorbitant; that poor locations are offered to minorities and that whites in general are promoting franchising as an extension of the servitude system. They further state that under the franchise concept, the whites are still in total control of the resources and minorities are still at the mercy of whites.

While I agree that franchising does have its problems, it still offers many good opportunities for minorities. In order to respond to minority criticism of franchising, we need to establish some sort of a national business development corporation that would focus on creating new enterprises which can be operated either on a franchise basis or on the chain concept. The key ingredient would be in minority control of the development corporation. This might very well be done through a joint venture arrangement with a corporation controlled by an experienced white firm.

A major shoe corporation, for example, might make available to the minority development corporation all of the expertise needed to start shoe stores with joint stock ownership between blacks and whites. As an incentive, the development corporation might agree to purchase shoes from the white corporation for its franchise or chain operation.

A hat corporation might establish for the development corporation stores which would sell shirts, ties, underwear, and hats. The hat corporation could provide very lenient inventory plans, as well as technical assistance, financial aid, and its own investment in the black development corporation.

Other such companies could participate likewise on a minority basis in a joint ownership which would franchise and/or chain-operate businesses to minorities.

There are many methods which might be used by the Institute for Economic Action. However, the key to the success of the minority enterprise effort is the need for someone to act as coordinator and stimulator.

In conclusion, let me try to explain the role of the Institute for Economic Action in terms of a metaphor. Everybody is sitting in the car, waiting to get going: the would-be black businessman, the business development organization, the banker. The Institute climbs into the driver's seat. The Institute is a chauffeur. He doesn't tell the passengers where they want to go, but once they tell him the destination, he is the professional who knows the best way to get there. He knows how fast he can go, where the potholes in the road are and how long it should take to get there. He is the one who finally gets the show on the road.

10   THE PUBLIC GOOD

We in America are inclined to talk about the "public sector" and the "private sector" as though they are sacred entities which, for chastity's sake, must be kept apart at all cost. That's the way we talk but, as in so many things, the way we act is quite different. The public sector invades the private and vice versa again and again and frequently to the advantage of both. The federal government bails out a bankrupt aerospace company, repairs a financially wrecked railroad, or deposits huge sums of money to refinance a failed bank. Dramatic—and expensive—rescues of this kind are becoming more and more common and the federal government unfailingly justifies the staggering expenditures required by arguing that they are in the public good: preserving jobs, maintaining interstate commerce, or reinforcing confidence in the banking system.

Fair enough. Those objectives are desirable. But isn't opening up opportunities for twenty-five million black Americans also in the public good, in fact, crucial to the public good? If the federal government can invest huge amounts of money in big businesses that bungled, why can't it invest similar sums of money in small businesses that never had a chance?

The federal government has been slow to recognize that by encouraging the growth of black business it can help not only many individuals but also invigorate the entire black community and therefore improve the social and economic health of the whole country. Even the Johnson administration, its other accomplishments in civil rights notwithstanding, never promoted black business ownership on a large scale, but simply supported many small programs directed at treating symptoms, not causes.

Perhaps it was appropriate that Richard Nixon, who was after all the standard bearer of the party traditionally associated with business, should take the first important step. During the 1968 presidential campaign, he promised in a series of speeches that he would see to it that the business of America included black business. He even offered the hopeful prognostication that "to the extent that programs of black capitalism are successful, ghettos will gradually disappear."

Less than two months after he took office, President Nixon made good his promise by signing Executive

Order 11458 which directed Secretary of Commerce Maurice H. Stans to establish within his department an Office of Minority Business Enterprise. "Encouraging increased minority group business activity," the President said in a statement accompanying the order, "is one of the priority aims of this administration." It was an historic statement. For the first time a President had formally recognized by executive order that the federal government had a responsibility to black business.

The President in fact charged the new office, generally referred to as OMBE, to do four things:

(1) To coordinate all programs in the public sector having a relevance to minority enterprise to make sure that there exists the most efficient utilization of available resources;

(2) To stimulate and mobilize the resources in the private sector so that the business community would direct a maximum share of its resources toward assisting minorities having an entrepreneurial desire;

(3) To establish a data bank to provide coordination for the massive flow of information in the public and private sector relating to minority enterprise. The data bank would be used to collect, analyze, and disseminate all pertinent minority enterprise data to and from local communities where it is needed and can be used; and

(4) To form an advisory council to provide private sector participation, guidance and counsel to the President and the Secretary of Commerce.

From the start, however, it was clear that OMBE was not going to be an immediate rags to riches success story. In fairness to Mr. Nixon, he did have other things on his mind, including a gloomy, sluggish economy. But OMBE simply did not receive either the consistent executive attention or the necessary funding to give credence to the promise that it would be one of the priorities of the administration. At the start only $1.2 million was set aside for the program. OMBE, moreover, had little authority to coordinate the many federal agencies actively engaged in minority enterprise efforts. Finally, many people in the black community complained that the whole program was developed within the White House and without the consultation or participation of capable leadership from the black community. OMBE was not off to a strong start.

It was not until two and one half years later that the President made a forceful effort on behalf of the program. In October 1971, he went to Congress and asked for $43.6 million for the remainder of the fiscal year and for an additional $63.6 million for the following fiscal year. The President said that 10 percent of that money would be used at the national level to strengthen minority business and trade associations, to generate broad private programs of marketing and financial assistance, to develop training programs and to foster other national efforts." "The remaining 90 percent of the new money would be spent on the local level—supporting a variety of efforts to identify, train, advise or assist minority businessmen, and to put them in touch with one another and with non-minority businessmen who can provide them with additional help." Certainly, this was the kind of commitment the program needed from the beginning.

With the 1968–1972 presidential term drawing to a close, the Nixon administration had at least accomplished some of OMBE's objectives:

The federal government greatly increased its business with minority-owned firms. The dollar value of goods and services purchased by federal agencies from minority firms rose from $13 million in fiscal 1969 to $30 million in 1970 to $142 million in 1971.

The government agreed to deposit $35 million of its own funds in minority banks and secured promises from major corporations to deposit $65 million of their money in minority banks.

The Small Business Administration licensed forty-six MESBICs (Minority Enterprise Small Business Investment Companies) with an aggregate capitalization of more than $10 million. When all of that money is fully used it should be able to generate an additional $150 million for the financing of minority business.

The Commerce Department spent $1 million to conduct the first nationwide survey of minority business ever made.

The Opportunity Funding Corporation received $7.4 million from the Office of Economic Opportunity to stimulate minority ownership programs.

In addition, OMBE deserves credit for helping to

convince private corporations, associations, and foundations to put their money, time, and effort into the
development of black business. Among these programs
were these:

The American Banking Industry increased its participation in federal loan programs during the period 1969
to 1971 by 31.4 percent. The dollar volume of the participation increased by nearly 89 percent.

The American Bankers Association instituted a $1
billion investment program which is designed to promote minority business development by increasing the
member banks' portfolio of minority business loans. A
survey is being conducted by the American Bankers
Association to determine the funds that have been allo-
cated to this program during its first year of operation.
Also, in a one-year training program, ABA is providing
forty minority trainees with on-the-job experience in
bank management.

The Commercial Banking Industry has established
an investment company "minibanc" to supply equity
capital to minority-owned banks. Minibanc will be capitalized at $10 million. Thirteen banks throughout the
country will participate in the initial private offering.

The franchise industry has increased the number of
minority-owned franchisees from 405 in 1969 to over
1,184 in 1971, an increase of more than 192 percent.

The life insurance industry, through its urban investment program, has invested a total of $87.8 million in
minority businesses through direct loans, deposits, in-

113

vestments and loan commitments. These investments are in the areas of commercial and industrial businesses, buildings, and bank deposits.

Fourteen of the largest professional and technical associations have made firm pledges to assist minority businessmen by furnishing them with no-cost management and technical assistance: American Institute of Certified Public Accountants; Investment Bankers Association; National Legal Aid and Defenders; U.S. Chamber of Commerce; National Association of Food Chains; American Institute of Industrial Engineers; National Association of Accountants; Lawyers Committee for Civil Rights Under Law; American Society for Personnel Administration; International Council of Shopping Centers; Menswear Retailers of America; National Society of Professional Engineers; National Association of Manufacturers; National Association of Purchasing Management.

The Menswear Retail Association provided 8,340 hours of voluntary assistance valued in excess of $130,000 to more than 150 minority-owned clothing stores.

The Menswear Retail Association assisted in establishing 61 new retail stores throughout the country. The stores in operation have retail sales that exceed $87 million.

Foundations have assisted the minority business effort by committing more than $47 million of their endowments to minority loans and investments.

For example in 1971:

The Ford Foundation made technical assistance grants to business development organizations amounting to $3,300,000 and $5 million in grants to community development corporations;

CNA Financial Foundation opened checking accounts into minority banks for half of their operating funds;

Taconic Foundation provided $150,000 to support a program to aid minority businessmen in obtaining financing.

Religious organizations have assisted minority business development as follows:

Episcopal Church Ghetto Investment Fund sponsored 11 business projects in the amount of $2,325,585;

United Methodist Church invested $2 million;

National Council of Churches of Christ Fund invested $260,000;

Presbyterian Economic Development Corporation invested $5 million and deposited $2 million in minority banks;

(Southern) Presbyterian Church in the United States has invested $150,000.

Through its Urban Affairs program the International Council of Shopping Centers has provided substantial assistance to three minority-owned shopping centers now in operation as well as three other centers now in various stages of construction. Fifteen or more projects are currently under review.

At the very least, all of this constitutes a beginning.

It means that a precedent has been established. The federal government has acknowledged that it has a responsibility for the encouragement and development of minority business and it has even initiated such imaginative programs as MESBIC. Nonetheless, the MESBIC program has suffered from serious shortcomings both in its efforts to provide minority businessmen with capital and in its attempts to guide them with technical assistance.

The MESBIC concept was designed to alleviate the minority community's chronic shortage of equity capital, that is, the money that the entrepreneur usually invests himself and which ordinarily stays in the business for the life of the business. Banks, as I pointed out before, do not invest equity capital. Banks make money by keeping the money moving. They do not want it to sit in any one business forever.

The truth is that the MESBICs have found themselves with the same necessity to keep the money moving. Consider, for example, what happens when a businessman comes to a MESBIC with a request for $100,000. If the MESBIC were to invest the entire amount itself and leave it in the business indefinitely, the MESBIC would soon deplete all of its funds and would be able to invest in very few ventures.

In most cases, therefore, the MESBIC commits itself for 20 percent, or $20,000. The balance of $80,000 comes from the bank and the SBA guarantees 90 percent so that the bank has only $8,000 of its own money extended without protection. But that doesn't solve the problem of the businessman who needs equity capital that can be left in the business.

MESBICs have tried to respond to this crucial need in the minority business community. They have even agreed, in many cases, to ask only for interest payments in the first year or so of business. In other cases they have agreed to conditions that were not part of the original contract, such as converting regular loans to equity investments to provide the minority entrepreneur with at least a slim chance of survival. But in the end it is always the same. Minority-owned businesses which have opened with the idea that borrowed funds would serve their need for equity capital have found themselves eyeball to eyeball with failure.

The primary ingredient that black businessmen lack is not loan capital. They need equity capital and up to this time there has not been much equity capital available to them. This need must be filled by someone and the most likely source is the federal government. One approach would be to establish an equity investment fund which could provide a minority businessman, once only, with the amount of equity capital that he needs to establish the proper debt-equity ratio and have a chance at success. Until this approach, or one like it, is considered by the federal government the MESBIC program will continue to be burdened with responsibilities that it cannot meet.

MESBICs have been frustrated by still another problem, their inability to provide technical assistance to a businessman until after he has opened his doors.

There must be more attention given to helping the minority businessman before he starts into business, before he has invested every penny he can beg, borrow and steal, only to find out that he has made the biggest mistake of his life. There are funds that could be used for such training. The Labor Department has a considerable amount of money at its disposal for training purposes. Most of this money, however, is earmarked for job training and Labor Department officials have interpreted "job training" to mean teaching the hard-core unemployed, the disadvantaged, or employees lacking the skills for a particular job.

Why shouldn't "job training" be interpreted to include the needy entrepreneur as well? In many instances black businessmen are worse off than their employees. They are slaves to businesses which do not give them even a decent salary. Therefore, the funds should be used to train not only the potential employees, but the potential employers as well.

Now that a start has been made, it is unlikely that the Nixon administration or any of its successors will turn its back on minority business. Much more likely, the program will continue to grow. The federal government, it is hoped, will also extend its authority and prestige to encourage black business development in other ways. For example, there are laws on the books prohibiting racial discrimination in the sale and rental of real estate, and yet black businessmen are discriminated against when they try to buy secure property in the most promising commercial neighborhoods. There are many other problems which could be resolved quickly if only the federal government would enforce existing laws prohibiting discrimination because of race or color. The law of the land must apply equally to all people.

The Nixon administration at one time set an ambitious and inspiring goal for minority ownership. The goal was nothing less than parity. In other words, the administration said that blacks and other minority people should own a percentage of the business community equivalent to our percentage of the population. The 17 percent of the business that minority people would own under such a goal should be, of course, 17 percent of the total sales and total assets of the business community rather than simply 17 percent of the business establishments. Owning 17 percent of the business establishments could come down to nothing more than possessing a collection of prehistoric, marginal mom-and-pop operations.

Neither the Nixon administration nor any other administration can provide such parity all by itself. That will require the combined efforts of all of the institutions and individuals that we enumerated throughout this book. But if a pledge to work toward parity means that the federal government keeps spending, lending, encouraging, coaxing, prodding, training, enforcing and won't rest until parity is achieved, then it's an intelligent and honest aim.

11 CONCLUSION

Where have we been and where are we going?

I began this book by acknowledging that black business is in serious trouble. In almost every case a black business is a tiny, dreary, and inefficient enterprise that consumes all of its owner's energy and rarely pays him off with more than a meager hand-to-mouth subsistence.

In the past few years it has become fashionable to be concerned about black business. Black people and white people talk about black business all the time—its present condition, its needs, its goals—and many people are sincerely trying to help. Unfortunately, at least a little of the effort is dishonest, much of it misguided, and almost all of it blurred by a dangerous mythology about business in general and black business in particular.

What then are the real issues, the real problems? Certainly, one of the most debilitating problems is this: The black businessman, long before he even dreamed of becoming a businessman, was deprived of essential knowledge and techniques that largely determine whether or not a businessman will make it. Throughout the two hundred-year period during which the American business system, the American way of doing things, was developed, expanded, and refined, black people were excluded by discrimination in hiring, by segregation in schools and even by housing patterns that determined that most black youngsters would grow up in communities where businessmen who might have been inspiring models of success turned into melancholy pictures of failure.

How does the black businessman catch up?

It would be foolhardy to underestimate the difficulty involved. The black man has to catch up with a system that is not only two hundred years ahead of him, but is also speeding away from him as it is continuously added to and improved. The black man, in effect, has to board a plane already in supersonic flight. But this is a resourceful country with large numbers of intelligent and concerned people, both black and white. This country put men on the moon. It can put black men and women in the American business system. I have suggested a number of ways.

The trade or business association can become a

school in which the black businessman can learn the most efficient techniques of the travel business, the real estate business, the insurance business, or practically any other business. Also, through the trade association many small businesses can become, in effect, a single big business in order to take advantage of such prerogatives as quantity purchasing and national advertising.

The franchise was another opportunity discussed in detail. A promising franchise offered by a reputable firm can serve more than one useful purpose. By offering a proven product or service it can generally assure the black businessman a moderately comfortable existence. But equally important is the training value of the franchise. In essence, a franchise is a system. The way of doing business has been pretested and determined before the franchisee cuts the ribbon for the grand opening. All of the details have been worked out—how much space to set aside for parking, how to display products, how large a staff to hire, how much to charge. The franchise is like the teaching machine that tells the entrepreneur every step of the way whether he is following correct procedures.

A poorly chosen franchise, however, can present insuperable problems, and I emphasize this point: the prospective franchisee must investigate the opportunity thoroughly before he commits himself.

Like the reputable franchise, the established business that someone else started and now wants to sell could represent an excellent opportunity. At its best, the established business can offer even more advantages than the franchise because it not only contains its own system within it, but has also attracted a clientele, established a reputation with creditors and adapted itself to its particular environment. The question that must be asked about the established business is whether it is simply a slightly used business or really a worn out business. To supply the answer we need a transfer agent, an honest broker who can stand between the white businessman who wants to sell and the black businessman who wants to buy. The transfer agent makes sure that the business is being sold at a fair price and that the black entrepreneur knows what he is getting into. The transfer agent should also help the black entrepreneur secure technical assistance. Ideally, the sale of the business might be spread out over a period of years so that the white businessman could teach systems and procedures to the black businessman during the transfer and also allow for a flexible formula of sale based on actual future earnings.

The nation's colleges and universities should assume a role in the development and encouragement of black business as well. The university is not only a repository for clear and inspired thinking but also a preserve for the enthusiasm of young people. If we can interest and engage those zealous students, black business will have an important ally for years to come.

Community organizations are important intermediaries between the individuals of the black community and the institutions of the white community. They can be extremely useful in making members of the black community aware of opportunities and also in helping entrepreneurs take advantage of those opportunities. Unfortunately, community organizations sometimes suffer from narrow thinking and an inclination to fall back on civil rights techniques. A sit-in is a dramatic and effective way to desegregate a luncheon counter, but it has absolutely nothing to do with purchasing a luncheon counter, operating it, or filling it with customers. In many cases, community organizations will have to rethink their procedures.

We need a national data bank, a clearinghouse of information where the names of black people who would make promising entrepreneurs can be kept on file and matched with proper opportunities. The man may be in Compton, California, and the opportunity that's right for him may be in Baltimore, Maryland. And we need an Institute for Economic Action that can serve as a guiding hand for the national development of black business.

We need the power and prestige and, let's face it, the financial resources of the federal government. We need administrations working for an honest parity.

What will we have at the end of it all?

Quite simply, black business will disappear. By that I mean that we will no longer have drab and gloomy, spirit-crushing, time-wasting, money-squandering black businesses that are doomed to live on the overlooked scraps of the economy. What we will have instead are healthy businesses that happen to be owned and operated by black people, but which do business with all 220 million Americans, not simply 25 million black Americans.

That is not an unrealistic goal. Its accomplishment does not even require the final evaporation of all bigotry, although, of course, the end of all racism is an ultimate goal. But black people can enjoy economic health even in the face of lingering bigotry. For example, anti-Semitism remains, sadly, a corruptive force in this country and yet, as far as I know, it doesn't stop many people from wearing Levis.

The success of the black entrepreneur will not put an end to all problems of black economic development. But it will help enormously. It will bring money into the black community to stay, money that can then be reinvested in the black community. And, just as important perhaps, the success of the businessman will be a source of pride for the black community, a vital confirmation that economic health is possible.

APPENDIX

Publications issued by the Small Business Guidance and Development Center, Howard University, Washington, D.C. 20001

Brochures	free
Ten Giant Steps	25¢ each; 10 for $2.00; 100 for $18.00
The Beauty Shop	$2.00
The Valet Service Establishment	$2.00
Student Essays on Small Businessmen	free
A Study of Self-Employment, Unemployment and the Inner City, Baltimore, Md.	free
Washington, D.C. Inner City Organizations Active in the Field of Minority Business and Economic Development	free
National Business League Joint Task Force for Minority Enterprise: a directory of organizations and programs active in the field of minority enterprise	free
Management Briefs (published ten times a year)	free

Publications Issued by the Institute for Minority Business Education, Howard University, Washington, D.C. 20001

Accessions (published ten times a year)	free
City Directories of Black Business	free
Manual for Organizing a Trade Association	$4.00
Manual for Establishing an Industrial Park in the Inner City	$4.00
Opportunities for Minorities	
Retail Trade: Industrial Profiles Series #1	$2.00
Services—Wholesale: Industrial Profiles Series #2	$2.00
Manufacturing: Industrial Profiles Series #3	$2.00
Negro in the Field of Business	$2.00
Profits	free

INDEX

National Association of Manufacturers, 114
National Association of Purchasing Management, 114
National Business League, 6, 44, 103
National Council of Churches of Christ Fund, 115
National Franchise Development Council, 104–105
National Institute of Dry Cleaners, 38
National Legal Aid and Defenders, 114
National Society of Professional Engineers, 114
Neighborhood Cleaners Association of New York City, 38
new business, transfer process in, 64–74
new models, business development organizations and, 99–107
Nixon, Richard M., 2, 109–112, 118–119
nonprofit corporations, in black business, 15
Northwest Airlines, 25
numbers, strength in, 33–44

Office of Economic Opportunity, 101
Office of Education, 101
Office of Minority Business Enterprise (OMBE), ix, 2–3, 101, 110–112
On the Job Training Program, 22
operational problems, in business development, 92–98

Opportunity Funding Corporation, 112
organization
    business, see business organization
    centralized national, 94
    local, 92–95

Parks, Henry, 6
Parks Sausage Company, 6
Parsons, Talcott, 27 n.
Pepsi-Cola Company, x
Philadelphia, black population and business in, 27–29
planning group, need for, 102
population, black business and, 27
Presbyterian Economic Development Corporation, 115
price competition, 29–30
pricing policy, 25, 84
Princeton University, ix
private sector, vs. public, 108–109
professional associations, investment and aid from, 114–115
professional careers, 22
Project BOSS, 103–104
promoter, role of, 91–92
promotion and delivery services, 90–98
Prudential Life Insurance Company, 90
public good, 108–119
public sector, vs. private, 108
purchasing economies, 35

quality control, 36–38, 84